ATHENS
In the Age of Pericles

The Centers of Civilization Series

ATHENS

In the Age of Pericles

By Charles Alexander Robinson, Jr.

NORMAN AND LONDON
UNIVERSITY OF OKLAHOMA PRESS

Library of Congress Catalog Card Number: 59-13472

ISBN: 0-8061-0935-1

Athens in the Age of Pericles is Volume 1 in *The Centers of Civilization Series*.

TO

MY DEAR WIFE

CELIA SACHS ROBINSON

WHO SHARES

THE JOYS AND TOIL

OF MY WORK

PREFACE

THIS BOOK is an essay on Athens in the fifth century B.C. I have tried to suggest in general terms based on exact scholarship the meaning of Periclean Athens, addressing my interpretation to laymen, in conformity with the style and length of the Centers of Civilization Series as envisaged by the University of Oklahoma Press. With the increasing mass of specialized research on ancient Athens, it is imperative to catch a general notion of the significance of the whole and moreover, if at all possible, to explain why it was Athens that became pre-eminent in contemporary Greece.

Periclean Athens is better understood, of course, if we know something of its background and its subsequent career, and for that reason I have indicated both the earlier and the later periods. But the emphasis is on the city at its height, and I have presented and assessed what is in my opinion the most characteristic. The result is a picture of a complex society, as any great civilization is bound to be, with its magnificent achievements and its faults. The ultimate failure of Athens is perhaps all the more arresting when we reflect that the Greeks reached their height and began their decline in the days of Pericles. So, at least, I believe. In these important matters it is well to stress what is inevitable and obvious, that the interpretation of a great era is admittedly subjective.

My manuscript has been read at different stages by two

friends, Professor Gilbert Highet of Columbia University and Professor C. Bradford Welles of Yale University. I extend to them my hearty thanks for their kind and generous help. The map of ancient Greece has been drawn by Mr. Erwin Raisz of the Institute of Geographical Exploration, Harvard University. I have used the following translations: Herodotus, by George Rawlinson; Thucydides and Plato's *Republic,* by Benjamin Jowett; the "Old Oligarch" and Xenophon's *Hellenica,* by H. G. Dakyns; Plato's *Symposium,* by Percy Bysshe Shelley; Aeschylus' *Prometheus Bound,* by Clarence W. Mendell (from his *Prometheus,* New Haven, Yale University Press, 1926); Sophocles' *Œdipus the King,* by David Grene (from his *Three Greek Tragedies in Translation,* Chicago, University of Chicago Press, 1942); *Œdipus at Colonus,* by E. H. Plumptre; *Antigone,* by Robert Whitelaw; Plutarch's *Pericles,* by Arthur Hugh Clough. I would also mention the great kindness and skill of Mrs. James J. Fine, who once again has typed my manuscript.

Charles Alexander Robinson, Jr.

Providence, Rhode Island

CONTENTS

ATHENS
In the Age of Pericles

I

STRIFE, FAITH, AND LIBERALITY

IN THE GLORIOUS fifth century before Christ, Greece was filled with a multitude of city-states, each of which was theoretically independent. Like many theories, this one was honored chiefly in the breach, but nevertheless it was the fierce love of autonomy that characterized the development of Greek civilization and helped bring mankind to a level of life that had never before been attained. When, however, it became clear that autonomy must yield to wider union, if the city-state was to survive as the driving force in Greek politics, the Greeks stubbornly refused to face reality and thereby made their own doom inevitable.

To explain these facts, which are among the most important questions ever asked of the Muse of History, is no less baffling than to state the essence of Greek civilization. This, at least, is true. Of all the Greek states that stretched so proudly from the Black Sea to the western shores of the Mediterranean, none approached Athens in magnificence, none could point to so large an empire or to such wealth and power, none possessed so pure and direct a democracy. The man primarily responsible for this vast achievement was Pericles, the leader of the Athenian democracy.

Plutarch, the biographer of the first century A.D., tells us that when Pericles lay on his deathbed the best of the citizens and those of his friends who were left alive came

3

and sat down beside him and spoke of the greatness of his merit and his power and reckoned up "his famous actions and the number of his victories; for there were no less than nine trophies, which, as their chief commander and conqueror of their enemies, he had set up for the honor of the city. Pericles, however, said that he wondered they should commend things which were as much owing to fortune as anything else and had happened to many other commanders, and at the same time should not speak of that which was the most excellent and greatest thing of all. 'For,' said he, 'no Athenian ever put on mourning because of me.' " It was an extraordinary boast, coming as it did from the man who set the stage for the collapse of Greek civilization as a whole, but what leader in history has not regarded himself as guiltless of his country's woes? Indeed, has any civilization ever reached its height without simultaneously sowing the seeds of its destruction? Is there not an almost incestuous relationship between dominion and decay?

A galaxy of brilliant men illumined Athens in the days before "the spring had gone out of the year." Their achievement marks one of the high points in the history of mankind, just as their failure to create an enduring society is man's greatest loss. The supreme question in history is to explain how any state reached great spiritual and intellectual heights. In antiquity the crown went to Athens, and the question must therefore be answered in Athenian terms.

Vibrancy, more than any other word, best describes Athens in the days of Pericles. The trade and commerce of its empire, and indeed of the entire Mediterranean, came to Piræus, Athens' harbor, and made the Athenians aware of strange people and products. The government

4

supported festivals with a magnificence and frequency unknown to the past and poured money into the construction of temples and other buildings. Intellectuals from abroad were attracted by the congenial atmosphere and settled in Athens to do their work.

It was the spirit of the people themselves, of course, that accounted for this. The Athenians apparently had no misgivings about their ability to manage their city and empire and were ever ready to experiment when a new problem called for a fresh solution. Success followed success and bred both confidence and an increasing boldness and arrogance. The time soon came when the Athenians equated the interests of the empire with their own and trampled upon their allies as they saw fit.

To explain how the Athenians became the leaders of Greece is, as we have already intimated, one of the challenging questions in history. Why the Greeks were gifted beyond normal mortals—why, among other things, they should have been surpassingly devoted to rationalism—is a wholly different question and perhaps can never be answered. Nor, probably, shall we ever be able to explain why the Greeks were the first to discover man, as Israel had God, and to insist on man's individual dignity and responsibility. As Protagoras put it, "Man is the measure of all things."

If, on the other hand, we now attempt to inquire how it came about that Athens, and not some other state, set the pace in the developing Greek culture, we should be able to find a reasonably satisfying answer in its past.

History proves abundantly that man long remembers former injustice and tyranny: Ireland and the American South leap to mind as modern illustrations. In ancient Greek history a cardinal fact was the so-called Dorian

Invasion of 1100 B.C., when the warlike Dorian Greeks entered Greece and overthrew the brilliant civilization of the Greek Bronze Age. Certain names—such as Mycenæ, Minoan Crete, and Troy—never again counted in history, for a new age, the classical period of Greece, was in the making. Wherever the Dorian Greeks settled in large numbers, there was bequeathed to posterity the memory of revolution and bloodshed.

Athens was spared this memory, for a battle on its frontiers deflected the Dorians southward, into the Peloponnesus. Needless to say, the Athenians had their share of problems, but racial hatred was not one of them. Perhaps it was because their problems were not so acute as to defy experimentation that the Athenians, alone among all Greeks, dared make their next crucial decision. We cannot be sure of the reasons for this, for we are still in the dim past when no contemporary records were kept, but the fact is that the people of Attica agreed to transfer their sovereignty to one place, Athens.

The characteristic political feature of historical Greece, the city-state, was a vigorously independent community. For example, in Bœotia, the district north from Attica, there were many such city-states, and we may speak of the people as Thebans and Thespians and so on, or collectively as Bœotians. But never may we speak of Atticans. The inhabitants of Eleusis, Marathon, Sunium, and the other towns of Attica were, all of them, Athenians.

Therefore, when we come into the relatively bright light of history, we find that, pressing though their many problems were, the people of Attica did not actively fear or hate one another, and in fact had been able to work out compromises resulting in the amalgamation of their state. Strife there always would be at Athens, between individuals and between classes, but it was not so fierce that there was no room to engage safely and effectively in another form of strife, intellectual creativity.

The ability to compromise may be accepted, without much argument, as a cornerstone of democracy, but it is something else to suggest that the opportunity for strife—and the participation in it, at a higher level than mere physical conflict—is vital for great intellectual achievement. The proof has always been so obvious that it may explain why it has not been seized upon to clarify the most profound enigma of all time, the decline of the Roman Empire.

During the second century A. D., under Hadrian and the Antonines, the Roman Empire brought the entire civilized Western world to unprecedented heights. Collapse lay immediately ahead, but in the meantime well-nigh universal peace and widespread prosperity reigned from Britain to Mesopotamia. This same century, as is well known, produced only a few great books (Lucian's, for example), no new principle in art, no significant scientific discovery, and, save in jurisprudence, few constructive ideas in government. Except in engineering, there was a complete stagnation of technique. This is surprising, especially when we recall that civilization began in Egypt and Mesopotamia with such inventions as irrigation works, writing, and the calendar.

It has been argued that the upper classes of the Roman Empire were responsible for this stagnation, because technical progress would have challenged a privileged position that rested on slavery and the tenant farmer. Complacency, however, will not stay confined to one aspect of life. During the second century it spread to literature, a field in which ancient man, and especially the aristocrat,

7

Reference map of

ANCIENT GREECE

Scale of Miles

0   100

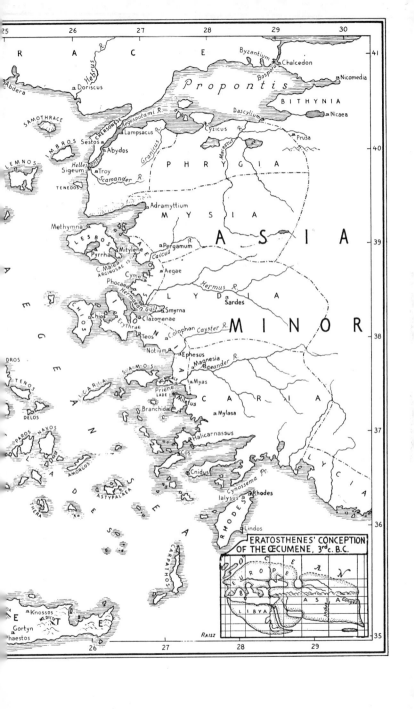

THRACE

25 · 26 · 27 · 28 · 29 · 30

41

Abdera · Doriscus

Byzantium · Chalcedon

Propontis

Bosporus · Nicomedia

BITHYNIA

SAMOTHRACE

CHERSONESE · Aegospotami R.

Dascylium

Nicaea

IMBROS · Sestos · Lampsacus

Cyzicus

Prusa

40

LEMNOS · Abydos · Hellespont

Granicus · PHRYGIA

Maeandrus

Sigeum · Troy

TENEDOS · Scamander R.

Adramyttium

MYSIA

ASIA

39

Methymna

LESBOS · Pergamum

Mitylene · Caicus R.

Pyrrha

C. Malea · Aegae

ARGINUSAE IS. · Cyme

Phocaea · Hermus R.

LYDIA

Hermean Gulf · Smyrna

Sardes

CHIOS · Chios · Clazomenae

Erythrae

MINOR

38

Teos · Colophon · Cayster R.

Notium

ANDROS · Ephesus

TENOS · SAMOS · Magnesia · Maeander R.

MYCALE · Myas

ICARIA · Priene

DELOS · LADE I. · Miletus

CARIA

37

PAROS · NAXOS · Branchidae

Mylasa

AMORGOS

Halicarnassus

HERA · Cos

ASTYPALAEA

Cnidus

Cynossema Pr.

36

SID · Ialysus · Rhodes

CARPATHOS

RHODES

Lindos

ERATOSTHENES' CONCEPTION
OF THE OECUMENE, 3rd c. B.C.

35

Knossos · MT. DICTE

CRETE

Gortyn · Phaestos

EUROPE · ASIA · N

LIBYA · ASIA

RAISZ

26 · 27 · 28 · 29

was often pre-eminent. Imitation now took the place of originality in literature, repetition destroyed initiative, form and style counted for more than thought and imagination. The audience was a narrow, educated one.

And yet, at the very same time within the same society, there developed a new literature, the Christian, which was full of vitality and was addressed to common folk as well as the cultivated few. Christian literature did this because it had to, if it was to survive. It was engaged in strife, strife with pagans, heretics, and government itself.

Strife, as we use it here, is but another word for faith in one's cause. The civilization of the Roman world was aristocratic, and when the upper classes refused to go forward, leadership fell to another element in the state. This is not to suggest that a society to be creative must be democratic, for there has never yet been a full and complete democracy anywhere. But there must exist in every society at least one class which is willing and able to strive toward the new; otherwise, stagnation affects the entire fabric.

Ancient Greece, and more particularly Athens, achieved what it did because its developing culture was carried by a larger percentage of its citizens. All Greek states, it is imperative to add, shared in the cultural advance, but Athens became the leader because the opportunity to experiment existed for several centuries and was seized upon by the people.

Some of this was due to accident, of course. The classical Athenians can take no credit for the fact that the Dorians did not conquer their ancestors, but the ensuing experimentation in which they engaged, entailing real strife as it did, must be chalked up in their favor.

First, as we have said, was the transference by every

town in Attica of its sovereignty to one place, Athens. Precisely the same intellectual breadth, again unique among Greek states, is met in 594 B.C., at the time of Solon's reforms. Athens was not yet important in the contemporary world. It was an agrarian state, and to strengthen it economically Solon decided to introduce manufactures. Since sufficient artisans—for the making of pots, mirrors, shields, and so on—did not exist in Athens, Solon persuaded his fellow citizens to invite them to come from abroad and, very especially, to grant them citizenship. This was necessary, if the invitation was to be accepted.

To appreciate the significance of this policy, we must bear in mind that no greater shock could possibly have been offered the citizens of any Greek state. The only way in which a man could be a citizen of a state was to be born in it, the free son of parents who had likewise been born in it. The unique action on the part of the Athenians in accepting Solon's proposal makes all else seem secondary.

It must have occurred to Solon, however, that if artisans flocked to Athens in any numbers, they would create a proletariat and become a force for democracy, as we would describe it, though the institution had not yet been invented. This was, in fact, very clear to Solon, for, in devising his instruments for limited self-government, he took a most exceptional step. Qualification for office was based on wealth, but heretofore wealth had been counted in bushels or measures—in the amount of wheat or oil or wine a man's farm produced. This was a conservative brake on the people, since the aristocracy owned the source of the wealth, the best land. Now Solon abandoned the old land qualification for one expressed in terms of

11

money. A growing city, increased prosperity, and the inevitable depreciation of the value of the coinage soon meant that all but the very poorest citizens could qualify for high office. This was the course of Athens during the sixth century.

Nothing short of strong faith in themselves could have led the Athenians to share the most precious gift in their possession—citizenship—with others. Such liberality and breadth of intellectual horizon produced a wonderful vibrancy and willingness to experiment, which by the end of the sixth century made possible Cleisthenes' democratic reforms. Corrections, elaborations, and even radical extensions would be made in future years, but the state had won the devotion of its people. If necessary, they were ready to fight on behalf of their institutions, and, as it happened, this they were soon called upon to do, as the Persian Empire steadily expanded westward.

Like other Greeks, the Athenians felt themselves different from, and superior to, the barbarians, as non-Greeks were called. The supposed difference between the Greeks and everyone else was caught delightfully and incisively by Herodotus of Halicarnassus. Herodotus wrote his history of the Persian Wars at Athens in the days of Pericles, but he had been born in Asia Minor and knew at first hand that complex world of many races which Persia had conquered. In telling the story of the conflict between Persia and Greece at the opening of the fifth century, he wished the reader to understand clearly the underlying issues and the nature of the contestants. Accordingly, he hit upon the device of describing a meeting between Solon and Crœsus, the incredibly rich Lydian king:

When all these conquests had been added to the

Lydian Empire, and the prosperity of Sardis was now at its height, there came thither, one after another, all the sages of Greece living at the time, and among them Solon, the Athenian. He was on his travels, having left Athens to be absent ten years, under the pretense of wishing to see the world, but really to avoid being forced to repeal any of the laws which, at the request of the Athenians, he had made for them. Without his sanction the Athenians could not repeal them, as they had bound themselves under a heavy curse to be governed for ten years by the laws which should be imposed on them by Solon.

On this account, as well as to see the world, Solon set out upon his travels, in the course of which he went to Egypt to the court of Amasis, and also came on a visit to Crœsus at Sardis. Crœsus received him as his guest, and lodged him in the royal palace. On the third or fourth day after, he bade his servants conduct Solon over his treasuries, and show him all their greatness and magnificence. When he had seen them all, and, so far as time allowed, inspected them, Crœsus addressed this question to him. "Stranger of Athens, we have heard much of thy wisdom and of thy travels through many lands, from love of knowledge and a wish to see the world. I am curious therefore to inquire of thee, whom, of all the men that thou hast seen, thou deemest the most happy?" This he asked because he thought himself the happiest of mortals: but Solon answered him without flattery, according to his true sentiments, "Tellus of Athens, sire." Full of astonishment at what he heard, Crœsus demanded sharply, "And wherefore dost thou deem Tellus happiest?" To which the other replied, "First, because his country was flourishing in his days, and he himself had sons both beautiful and good, and he lived to see children born to each of them, and these

13

children all grew up; and further because, after a life spent in what our people look upon as comfort, his end was surpassingly glorious. In a battle between the Athenians and their neighbors in Eleusis, he came to the assistance of his countrymen, routed the foe, and died upon the field most gallantly. The Athenians gave him a public funeral on the spot where he fell, and paid him the highest honors."

Thus did Solon admonish Crœsus by the example of Tellus, enumerating the manifold particulars of his happiness. When he had ended, Crœsus inquired a second time, who after Tellus seemed to him the happiest, expecting that at any rate, he would be given the second place. "Cleobis and Bito," Solon answered; "they were of Argive race; their fortune was enough for their wants, and they were besides endowed with so much bodily strength that they had both gained prizes at the Games. Also this tale is told of them:—There was a great festival in honor of the goddess Hera at Argos, to which their mother must needs be taken in a car. Now the oxen did not come home from the field in time: so the youths, fearful of being too late, put the yoke on their own necks, and themselves drew the car in which their mother rode. Five and forty furlongs did they draw her, and stopped before the temple. This deed of theirs was witnessed by the whole assembly of worshipers, and then their life closed in the best possible way. Herein, too, God showed forth most evidently, how much better a thing for man death is than life. For the Argive men, who stood around the car, extolled the vast strength of the youths; and the Argive women extolled the mother who was blessed with such a pair of sons; and the mother herself, overjoyed at the deed and at the praises it had won, standing straight before the image, besought the goddess to bestow on Cleobis and Bito, the sons who had so mightily honored her, the highest blessing to which mortals can attain. Her prayer ended, they offered sacrifice and partook of the holy banquet, after which the two youths fell asleep in the temple. They never woke more, but so passed from the earth. The Argives, looking on them as among the best of men, caused statues of them to be made, which they gave to the shrine at Delphi."

When Solon had thus assigned these youths the second place, Crœsus broke in angrily, "What, stranger of Athens, is my happiness, then, so utterly set at nought by thee, that thou dost not even put me on a level with private men?"

"Oh! Crœsus," replied the other, "thou askedst a question concerning the condition of man, of one who knows that the power above us is full of jealousy, and fond of troubling our lot. A long life gives one to witness much, and experience much oneself, that one would not choose. Seventy years I regard as the limit of the life of man. In these seventy years are contained, without reckoning intercalary months, twenty-five thousand and two hundred days. Add an intercalary month to every other year, that the seasons may come round at the right time, and there will be, besides the seventy years, thirty-five such months, making an addition of one thousand and fifty days. The whole number of the days contained in the seventy years will thus be twenty-six thousand two hundred and fifty, whereof not one but will produce events unlike the rest. Hence man is wholly accident. For thyself, oh! Crœsus, I see that thou art wonderfully rich, and art the lord of many nations; but with respect to that whereon thou questionest me, I have no answer to give, until I hear that thou hast closed thy life happily. For assuredly he who possesses great store of riches is no nearer happiness than he who has what suffices for his daily needs, unless it so hap that luck attend upon him, and so he continue in the enjoyment of all his good things to the end of life. For many of the wealthiest men have been unfavored of fortune, and many whose means were moderate have had excellent luck. Men of the former class excel those of the latter but in two respects; these last excel the former in many. The wealthy man is better able to content his desires, and to bear up against a sudden buffet of calamity. The other has less ability to withstand these evils (from which, however, his good luck keeps him clear), but he enjoys all these following blessings: he is whole of limb, a stranger to disease, free from misfortune, happy in his children, and comely to look upon. If, in addition to all this, he end his life well, he is of a truth the man of whom thou art in search, the man who may rightly be termed happy. Call him, however, until he die, not happy but fortunate. Scarcely, indeed, can any man unite all these advantages: as there is no country which contains within it all that it needs, but each, while it possesses some things, lacks others, and the best country is that which contains the most; so no single human being is complete in every respect— something is always lacking. He who unites the greatest number of advantages, and retaining them to the day of his death, then dies peaceably, that man alone, sire, is, in my judgment, entitled to bear the name of 'happy.' But in every matter it behoves us to mark well the end: for oftentimes God gives men a gleam of happiness, and then plunges them into ruin."

Such was the speech which Solon addressed to Crœsus, a speech which brought him neither largess nor honor. The king saw him depart with much indifference, since he thought that a man must be an arrant fool who made no account of present good, but bade men always wait and mark the end.

Sophocles, in his *Œdipus the King*, also insisted that we must mark well the end:

> Look upon that last day always. Count no mortal happy till he has passed the final limit of his life secure from pain.

But, of course, what really mattered was the manner of life a man pursued through all his years. Herodotus makes clear the simplicity and the directness of Greek life, the glory of the simple virtues, the rewards of courage, the easy intercourse between men, and the high regard for the gods. He wished us to believe that in these matters the East and West did not see eye to eye, that it was the West that placed an emphasis on intangibles.

As these ideals became clouded, or were replaced by different ones, the other side of human nature came more and more to the front. For there can be little doubt that no people in history has been more tyrannical and cruel than the Athenians at certain moments. So complex and contradictory apparently is man, and the men of Athens will never be fully understood unless we bear both sides of the coin in mind.

II

THE STRENGTH OF THE DEMOCRACY

THE GLORIOUS FIFTH century B. C. opened with a deep international crisis. The Persian Empire, typically eastern in its predatory nature, having conquered the Greeks of Asia Minor, now advanced against Greece itself. Athens, alone among the important Greek states, felt sure enough of itself to stand against the Persians at Marathon (490 B. C.). They were the first among the Greeks ever to gaze victoriously on the Persians. Ten years later, to be sure, the Spartan king, Leonidas, made his immortal stand at Thermopylæ, but all those with him were killed. It was the strategy of the Athenian upstart, Themistocles, that saved the day. He had had the vision to see that a vast Persian host could not maintain itself in Greece without a supporting fleet. Therefore, at his urging, the Athenians built the fleet that completely routed the Persians in the Bay of Salamis, off Athens.

The enthusiasm of the Athenians is easy to understand. They had saved Greek civilization, and as we now know, European civilization, from Oriental conquest. No long time passed before the Athenians urged other states to join in a defensive alliance or confederacy against another possible Persian invasion.

The states that accepted Athens' suggestion were chiefly in Asia Minor, for they had only just now been freed from Persia. And the islands of the Ægean Sea also joined, since a new Persian fleet might pick them off one by one.

Every state paid its share—either with ships or money—toward the common defense, but in time Athens became the actual head and used any surplus money as she wished. The fleet, too, became almost exclusively hers.

Athens had been willing to fight for freedom and had fought successfully. And then she seized the opportunity of empire. The empire, beginning as a confederacy, stretched across the Aegean Sea and was dependent on the Athenian fleet. The fleet was dependent on its rowers, the poorest members of the state. Hence the poorest Athenians more and more dominated the government, more and more they shared in its benefits, more and more they helped shape the development of its civilization. The person primarily responsible for creating the Athenian Empire and for making the masses feel that they had a stake in the future was, like Solon, a noble, Pericles, the son of Xanthippus, a member of Athens' most famous clan, the Alcmæonid. With him democracy and imperialism went hand in hand.

Athens won her empire, as she did her leadership in the developing Greek culture, because at different times in different ways she took a chance, now ready to compromise and amalgamate the state, now eager to grant citizenship to foreign artisans who would produce a new prosperity, now determined to fight for freedom. As the historian, Thucydides expressed it, the Athenians made "every sea and land a highway of their daring." And yet, though they never hesitated to vote themselves benefits, the Athenians resolutely refused to share them with their allies in the empire. It is customary to say that autonomy was so deeply rooted in Greece that the allies, for example, would not have accepted Athenian citizenship if offered, but we have no way of knowing this.

What we do know is that the masses, conscious of their power in the fleet and hence in the empire, demanded that their leaders conduct affairs more and more on their behalf. There were two sides to this, however, for when we lift our sights and focus on the international crises, the unselfish attitude of the masses stands out in sharp relief. Ancient Greece had only three international crises: the Persian, the Macedonian (represented by Philip and Alexander), and the final overwhelming one, the Roman. There is little doubt that in the first crisis, and none whatever in the two following, the ordinary folk supported the patriot cause and fought the enemy, while the rich were willing to accept foreign rule if that was necessary to prevent social revolution.

With profound insight Thucydides tells us that enslavement to the opposite political faction in one's state is "worse than the domination of a foreigner." There, of course, is the explanation of the particularly fierce and cruel character of all civil wars. In ancient Greece, the only persistent political issue running throughout its history was the struggle between the Few and the Many, and it was a rare moment when the twin cries, demanding the cancellation of debts and the redistribution of property, were not heard in every state.

The rich, accordingly, turned to the foreigner, when they could, to preserve the status quo or to alter it in their interest. This was seldom enough, and in between times they strove to maintain their position or to upset the democrats by assassination, political clubs, and pamphleteering. Not all the rich, suffice it to say, were enemies of the Athenian democracy, but so far as there was organized opposition to the constitution it lay in that quarter.

There has survived from antiquity an extraordinary

document, known as *The Constitution of the Athenians,* which reveals the danger posed by a class of rich and intelligent men. It was written not long after the outbreak of the conflict between Athens and Sparta, known as the Peloponnesian War, by a person who is best called "The Old Oligarch." Although the Old Oligarch equates those of like mind with the "better" citizens and the democrats with the "worse," he has actually succeeded in painting the strength of the Athenian democracy:

Now, as for the constitution of the Athenians, and the type or manner of constitution which they have chosen, I praise it not, in so far as the very choice involves the welfare of the baser folk as opposed to that of the better class. I repeat, I withhold my praise so far; but, given the fact that this is the type agreed upon, I propose to show that they set about its preservation in the right way; and that those other transactions in connection with it, which are looked upon as blunders by the rest of the Hellenic world, are the reverse.

In the first place, I maintain, it is only just that the poorer classes and the common people of Athens should be better off than the men of birth and wealth, seeing that it is the people who man the fleet, and have brought the city her power. The steersman, the boatswain, the lieutenant, the look-out-man at the prow, the shipwright—these are the people who supply the city with power far rather than her heavy infantry and men of birth and quality. This being the case, it seems only just that offices of state should be thrown open to every one both in the ballot and the show of hands, and that the right of speech should belong to any one who likes, without restriction. For, observe, there are many of these offices which, according as they are in good or in bad hands, are a source of safety or of danger to the People, and in these the People prudently abstains from sharing; as, for instance, it does not think it incumbent on itself to share in the functions of the general or of the commander of cavalry. The commons recognizes the fact that in foregoing the personal exercise of these offices, and leaving them to the control of the more powerful citizens, it secures the balance of advantage to itself. It is only those departments of government which bring pay and assist the private estate that the People cares to keep in its own hands.

In the next place, in regard to what some people are puzzled to explain—the fact that everywhere greater consideration is shown to the base, to poor people and to common folk, than to persons of good quality,—so far from being a matter of surprise, this, as can be shown, is the keystone of the preservation of the democracy. It is these poor people, this common folk, this worse element, whose prosperity, combined with the growth of their numbers, enhances the democracy. Whereas, a shifting of fortune to the advantage of the wealthy and the better classes implies the establishment on the part of the commons of a strong power in opposition to itself. In fact, all the world over, the cream of society is in opposition to the democracy. Naturally, since the smallest amount of intemperance and injustice, together with the highest scrupulousness in the pursuit of excellence, is to be found in the ranks of the better class, while within the ranks of the People will be found the greatest amount of ignorance, disorderliness, rascality,—poverty acting as a stronger incentive to base conduct, not to speak of lack of education and ignorance, traceable to the lack of means which afflicts the average of mankind.

The objection may be raised that it was a mistake

to allow the universal right of speech and a seat in council. These should have been reserved for the cleverest, the flower of the community. But here, again, it will be found that they are acting with wise deliberation in granting to even the baser sort the right of speech, for supposing only the better people might speak, or sit in council, blessings would fall to the lot of those like themselves, but to the commons the reverse of blessings. Whereas now, anyone who likes, any base fellow, may get up and discover something to the advantage of himself and his equals. It may be retorted, "And what sort of advantage either for himself or for the People can such a fellow be expected to hit upon?" The answer to which is, that in their judgment the ignorance and the baseness of this fellow, together with his good will, are worth a great deal more to them than your superior person's virtue and wisdom, coupled with animosity. What it comes to, therefore, is that a state founded upon such institutions will not be the best state; but, given a democracy, these are the right means to secure its preservation. The People, it must be borne in mind, does not demand that the city should be well governed and itself a slave. It desires to be free and to be master. As to bad legislation it does not concern itself about that. In fact, what you believe to be bad legislation is the very source of the People's strength and freedom. But if you seek for good legislation, in the first place you will see the cleverest members of the community laying down the laws for the rest. And in the next place, the better class will curb and chastise the lower orders; the better class will deliberate in behalf of the state, and not suffer crack-brained fellows to sit in council, or to speak or vote in the assemblies. No doubt; but under the weight of such blessings the People will in a very short time be reduced to slavery.

Another point is the extraordinary amount of license granted to slaves and resident aliens at Athens, where a blow is illegal, and a slave will not step aside to let you pass him in the street. I will explain the reason of this peculiar custom. Supposing it were legal for a slave to be beaten by a free citizen, or for a resident alien or freedman to be beaten by a citizen, it would frequently happen that an Athenian might be mistaken for a slave or an alien and receive a beating; since the Athenian People is not better clothed than the slave or alien, nor in personal appearance is there any superiority. Or if the fact itself that slaves in Athens are allowed to indulge in luxury, and indeed in some cases to live magnificently, be found astonishing, this too, it can be shown, is done of set purpose. Where you have a naval power dependent upon wealth we must perforce be slaves to our slaves, in order that we may get in our slave-rents, and let the real slave go free. Where you have wealthy slaves it ceases to be advantageous that my slave should stand in awe of you.

The common people put a stop to citizens devoting their time to athletics and to the cultivation of music, disbelieving in the beauty of such training, and recognizing the fact that these are things the cultivation of which is beyond its power. On the same principle, in the case of the choregia, the management of athletics, and the command of ships, the fact is recognized that it is the rich man who trains the chorus, and the People for whom the chorus is trained; it is the rich man who is naval commander or superintendent of athletics, and the People that profits by their labors. In fact, what the People looks upon as its right is to pocket the money. To sing and run and dance and man the vessels is well enough, but only in order that the People may be the gainer, while the rich are made poorer. And so in the courts of justice, justice is not more an object of concern to the jurymen than what touches personal advantage.

To speak next of the allies, and in reference to the point that emissaries from Athens come out, and, according to common opinion, calumniate and vent their hatred upon the better sort of people, this is done on the principle that the ruler cannot help being hated by those whom he rules; but that if wealth and respectability are to wield power in the subject cities the empire of the Athenian People has but a short lease of existence. This explains why the better people are punished with infamy, robbed of their money, driven from their homes, and put to death, while the baser sort are promoted to honor. On the other hand, the better Athenians protect the better class in the allied cities. And why? Because they recognize that it is to the interest of their own class at all times to protect the best element in the cities. It may be urged that if it comes to strength and power the real strength of Athens lies in the capacity of her allies to contribute their money quota. But to the democratic mind it appears a higher advantage still for the individual Athenian to get hold of the wealth of the allies, leaving them only enough to live upon and to cultivate their estates, but powerless to harbor treacherous designs.

As to wealth, the Athenians are exceptionally placed with regard to Hellenic and foreign communities alike, in their ability to hold it. For, given that some state or other is rich in timber for shipbuilding, where is it to find a market for the product except by persuading the ruler of the sea? Or, suppose the wealth of some state or other to consist of iron, or may be of bronze, or of linen yarn, where will it find a market except by permission of the supreme maritime power? Yet these are the very things, you see, which I need for my ships. Timber I must have from one, and from another iron, from a third bronze, from a fourth linen yarn, from a fifth wax. Besides which they will not suffer their antagonists in those parts to carry these products elsewhere, or they will cease to use the sea. Accordingly I, without one stroke of labor, extract from the land and possess all these good things, thanks to my supremacy on the sea; while not a single other state possesses the two of them.

There is just one thing which the Athenians lack. Supposing they were the inhabitants of an island, and were still, as now, rulers of the sea, they would have had it in their power to work whatever mischief they liked, and to suffer no evil in return (as long as they kept command of the sea), neither the ravaging of their territory nor the expectation of an enemy's approach. Whereas at present the farming portion of the community and the wealthy landowners are ready to cringe before the enemy overmuch, while the People, knowing full well that, come what may, not one stock or stone of their property will suffer, nothing will be cut down, nothing burnt, lives in freedom from alarm, without fawning at the enemy's approach. Besides this, there is another fear from which they would have been exempt in an island home—the apprehension of the city being at any time betrayed by their oligarchs and the gates thrown open, and an enemy bursting suddenly in. How could incidents like these have taken place if an island had been their home? Again, had they inhabited an island there would have been no stirring of sedition against the People; whereas at present, in the event of faction, those who set it on foot base their hopes of success on the introduction of an enemy by land. But a people inhabiting an island would be free from all anxiety on that score. Since, however, they did not chance to inhabit an island from the first, what they now do is this—they deposit their property in the islands, trusting to their command of the sea, and they suffer the soil of Attica to be ravaged without a sigh. To expend pity on that, they know, would be to deprive themselves of other blessings still more precious.

Further, states oligarchically governed are forced to ratify their alliances and solemn oaths, and if they fail to abide by their contracts, the offence, by whomsoever committed, lies nominally at the door of the oligarchs who entered upon the contract. But in the case of engagements entered into by a democracy it is open to the People to throw the blame on the single individual who spoke in favor of some measure, or put it to the vote, and to maintain to the rest of the world, "I was not present, nor do I approve of the terms of the agreement." Inquiries are made in a full meeting of the People, and should any of these things be disapproved of, they can at once discover countless excuses to avoid doing whatever they do not wish. And if any mischief should spring out of any resolutions which the People has passed in council, the People can readily shift the blame from its own shoulders. "A handful of oligarchs acting against the interests of the People have ruined us." But if any good result ensue, they, the People, at once take the credit of that to themselves.

I repeat that my position concerning the constitution of the Athenians is this: the type of constitution is not to my taste, but given that a democratic form of government has been agreed upon, they do seem to me to go the right way to preserve the democracy by the adoption of the particular type which I have set forth.

A potent reason for the strength of democracy at Athens was the confidence of its citizens. Nor were there any second-class citizens, as we might express it. This had not been immediately true of the foreigners who, availing themselves of Solon's reforms, had settled in Athens and received citizenship, because they were, both socially and politically, not quite the equal of the old-time citizens, those of "pure" descent. At the end of the sixth century B.C., therefore, when he resumed the democratic march at Athens and set up the constitution which was to reach its full flowering under Pericles, the reformer Cleisthenes took cognizance of the unfortunate position of the "new" citizens. He abolished (except for certain ceremonial purposes) the four ancient Ionian tribes and substituted ten new ones in their place. Henceforth membership in a tribe, and with it the right to vote, had nothing to do with birth, kinship, or religion; membership in a particular tribe depended on residence, on whether or not a man lived in this or that deme (the smallest political unit, corresponding roughly to one of our wards).

The "new" citizen was generally an artisan who spent his time in the shops or on the streets of the city, but now he felt fully the equal of the farmer, the owner of land, who so often in history has enjoyed a presumed superiority. Cleisthenes made it possible for Athens to enter its great fifth century, when the threat of Persia loomed, with the people determined to advance their own interests. Probably the chief conservative brake was the absence of pay for continuous participation in the Assembly and juries, but the fact that the Assembly met in Athens made it easier for the artisan to attend than the farmer.

There was a tendency among the Athenians, moreover, to choose their leaders from among the great families, whose members in the past had successfully led the state and presumably would do so again. Republican Rome was given far more to this habit and indeed during the half century after the victory over Hannibal elected the overwhelming majority of its consuls from families who had previously held the office. The reason is not far to seek. At Rome the members of the Assembly voted directly on a question, ordinarily without debate, whereas in Athens debate was customary. Thus a man, with no family connections whatever, could urge a particular policy and win a position for himself among his fellow citizens. So difficult is it, however, to create a "perfect" constitution that this very freedom of debate, in the days when Pericles' restraining hand was gone, led to the rise of demagogues. Now a man, holding no office, could persuade the Assembly to adopt a policy thoroughly disapproved by the magistrates.

The energizing of the body politic at Athens—the high political spirit, the patriotism and confidence of the people —can be better understood by the depth of participation by the citizens in the city's life. Not only did the state have its political functions and festivals, but the ten tribes and the many demes supported their own as well. The ordinary man's opportunity for political development and education was immense. The idea of *sophrosyne,* self-restraint, inevitably grew apace, and with it a greater humanity and a betterment in the condition of women and the treatment of prisoners of war.

Æschylus, the great tragic poet, glowed with a passion for freedom and preached that justice must be tempered with mercy. He could not believe that the aristocrat was necessarily good and the poor bad, but on the contrary gave his sympathy to the lowly. Despite the oligarchical leanings of many of their fellow citizens. Æschylus and other aristocrats took the lead in the development of the arts and the democratization of the Athenian constitution. The masses of the people responded responsibly to their opportunity and produced military, artistic, intellectual, and political results which can only be described as prodigious. As Æschylus himself knew, the spirit of the Athenians was not easy to define, and perhaps it is still impossible to define it, but he probably came as close to an answer as we shall ever get. In his play, *The Persians,* which is an eye-witness account of the Battle of Salamis, the Persian queen asks a question more profound than she could possibly have guessed, "What is this Athens, of which all men speak?" And certainly she never understood the answer, "They bow to no man and are no man's slaves."

III

AN IMPERIAL DEMOCRACY

THIRTY YEARS after the end of the Persian Wars—precisely in the year 449 B.C.—it was clear to everyone that the immediate threat of another Persian invasion had passed and that the Greeks were free to work out their destiny. Accordingly, many of Athens' allies in the confederacy, which had been built up against Persia, could see no reason for continuing their contributions to the common treasury and stopped them altogether. Pericles, who had succeeded to the leadership at Athens a dozen years earlier, was of a different mind and persuaded his fellow citizens to enforce the payment of the tribute. He told the people that, so long as they provided protection against Persia, they might spend any surplus money as they wished, and that the time had long since come to rebuild the temples destroyed by the Persians, in accordance with their vows. As Plutarch put it, Pericles now set about adorning Athens like a vain woman, draping around her neck precious stones and statues and temples, for he taught the people that, since they protected the allies, they did not need to give them any reckoning.

It was in this way that a confederacy, formed for self-protection, was turned into the Athenian Empire. Few of the so-called allies dared demur, for the previous decades had revealed an increasingly savage reaction on Athens' part when any state had made an attempt to leave the confederacy.

There is no doubt that the imperial tribute made possible at Athens the erection of the Parthenon and other buildings, the many festivals, and the payment for various public services, thus affording an uncritical posterity, when motivated by crass materialism, with a justification for imperialism. When, however, we turn from the number of temples built, and the relative ease with which it was all accomplished, when we concentrate, rather, on the quality of the works created, it becomes clear that neither empire nor great wealth are necessary for spiritual and intellectual achievement. For example, Æschylus, who was perhaps the greatest of Greek dramatists, died half a dozen years before the birth of the Athenian Empire. A decade earlier still, Panhellenic efforts had raised the great temple of Zeus at Olympia, a marvelous portrayal in architecture and sculpture of grandeur itself, and the equal of the Parthenon in every respect except for certain technical matters.

Creativity might coincide with imperialism, but clearly it was independent of it. Nevertheless, Athenian imperialism had been born and was long to continue. Nor is there any denying its magnificent fruits for a limited period. In Athens itself there was little difference of opinion about the empire—whether to keep it or not—for the conservatives recognized that no politician could survive who opposed it. Its revenues tempted the masses far too much for that. It was in domestic politics, rather, that a sharp cleavage existed between the political factions. The conservatives held that Athens possessed neither the man power nor the wealth to oppose herself simultaneously to Persia by sea and Sparta by land, and they therefore urged a close association with Sparta.

The natural sympathies of the Athenian conservatives

lay with oligarchical Sparta, and there was, besides, much to be said for their position. In addition to the sturdy maritime empire, Pericles had created an empire by land, destined for a very brief life, but during its existence sufficient to terrify Sparta, its important commercial ally Corinth, and the rest of their Peloponnesian League. Could Athens, the conservatives asked, not only build a greater empire than the Peloponnesians, but also ruin their markets? Eastward, the Ægean Sea was already an Athenian lake, when Pericles seized Pegæ, a port on the Corinthian Gulf to which Athens could easily send goods overland for shipment to the west. Worse than that, Pericles seized Naupactus, a veritable Gibraltar at the west end of the gulf, controlling its entrance, so that henceforth the ships of Corinth came and went at the pleasure of Athens. It was at this moment, Thucydides remarks, that the Corinthians conceived an extreme hatred for Athens.

Pericles, on the other hand, maintained that Athens could go it alone and hurt the pride and trade of the Peloponnesians with impunity and, if necessary, fight both Sparta and Persia. The party warfare was understandably fierce, and to entrench his own position, Pericles proposed, first, that the jurors be paid for their service. Juries are probably the cornerstone of any democracy, and at Athens no less than six thousand jurors were selected every year. By giving them a daily wage, Pericles completely democratized the juries, since now even the poorest members could serve regularly. Indeed, the typical juror was an old man, and Pericles' proposal was in effect a form of old-age pension.

Pericles' second proposal was of a different order altogether, though like the first it too was passed. Athenian

citizenship, he argued, was rapidly becoming a prized possession, and there would be an advantage in restricting
it to as few as possible. He suggested to the Athenians,
therefore, that they limit the franchise to those who could
prove citizenship on both sides of the family. Five thousand names were now struck eagerly from the citizen lists.
This represented a complete reversal of Solon's farseeing
reform a century and a half earlier and brings us up
sharply against a fundamental question asked by Athenian history. Since Solon was followed by greatness, as
Pericles was by disaster, are we to conclude that liberality
and breadth of outlook produce the one, selfishness and
narrowness the other?

In such ways as we have described, Pericles broke the
conservative opposition to him. He was able to do so because, from the time of his emergence as leader of the
democratic faction in 461 B.C. to his death in 429 B.C.,
the Athenians elected him frequently to the Board of Ten
Generals, the chief executive body at Athens. Athens now
presents the picture of a state where the citizens elected
the magistrates—in a word, we seem to have a true democracy—and it is customary to let it go at that, in order
that ancient Greece may shine in as bright colors as possible. But we must not gloss over a startling statement of
the first importance by Thucydides, that as long as Pericles lived, "Athens, though still in name a democracy, was
in fact ruled by her first citizen." What could be the basis
for Thucydides' remark, or rather what had happened to
make such a remark possible? How could one-man rule
have overtaken a democracy?

It is quite true that when they wished, as occasionally
they did, the Athenians might not elect Pericles to high
office, but generally and enthusiastically they returned

him to the Board of Ten Generals. They gained confidence from his earnest manner, the majesty of his person, the dignity of his eloquence, his wisdom and incorruptibility. By the sheer force of his personality and his long experience on the Board of Ten Generals, he dominated the development of Athens during three critical decades.

In effect, this amounted to a perversion of the Athenian democracy, a terrifying fate, almost mysterious in its working, that has so often befallen a democratic constitution. At the opening of the fifth century B. C. it would have been impossible at Athens. In those days, before Marathon, the chief executive body had been the nine archons. Re-election was forbidden. But then, after the victory and as a new Persian invasion threatened, Themistocles thought he saw, as indeed he did, the measures Athens must take for salvation. Driven by both personal ambition and patriotism, as is generally the case with great leaders, he hoped to convince the Athenians that they must build a large fleet. But how was he to do this, since he had already been archon and could never be again?

As a first step, Themistocles decided to destroy, if not the office of archon itself, at least its power. Playing on the democratic temper of the day, he persuaded the Athenians to leave the selection of archons to the gods and to throw the archonship open to the lot. The only result of this could be that henceforth the archons would be nonentities. Inevitably, power at Athens would fall to another executive body, the Board of Ten Generals, where re-election was allowed. It was in this fashion that Themistocles was able to direct Athenian politics during the decade following Marathon, and though our ancient sources fail us in all the details, no other reconstruction will stand up.

At any rate, the archonship ceased to have any importance, except an honorary one, and executive leadership at Athens passed to a different board, that of the Ten Generals. Themistocles' vision saved Greece at Salamis, to be sure, but it was his crafty political maneuvering that upset the constitution. The implications were not immediately realized, but nevertheless the possibility of one-man rule at Athens had been opened.

The Ten Generals at Athens in the days of Pericles were elected, one from each of the ten tribes, by the citizens for a term of one year. Immediate re-election was possible. Their function was far more than a military one since, as the chief executive, they had the duty of presiding at the Assembly, advising the people on a course of action, and carrying out the more important decisions. The members of the Assembly were not experts in government, but ordinary men, eighteen years of age or over, who spent their lives as farmers or artisans or sailors. To guide them in their deliberations could not have been an easy task, especially since self-seeking demagogues might advocate policies in which the magistrates had no confidence.

With their customary directness, the Athenians saw to it that proposals in the first instance were carefully considered by the Council. This was a body of five hundred men selected annually by lot from the citizens who were over thirty years of age. Fifty were chosen from each of the ten tribes, and their collective responsibility was to prepare the agenda for the meeting of the Assembly.

Forty times a year—somewhat better than every ten days—the people gathered on a hill known as the Pnyx, just west of the Acropolis. These were bound to be electric occasions, demanding a consideration of domestic and foreign politics, problems of empire, the possibility of war.

Naturally, the city masses dominated the Assembly, since it was easiest for them to attend, and, what is not so generally known, they also had a decisive voice in the deliberations of the Council and thus in the proposals brought before the Assembly. A curious but effective means of proportional representation had been devised for the Council, whereby the fifty councillors of each tribe were chosen from the demes (or "wards") of the tribe on the basis of their population. Thus, as Athens grew, the city demes counted for more and more in the composition of the Council.

It would be a mistake to compare Periclean Athens with a New England town meeting, since the issues and responsibility were so very different, and yet each in its own way represented a simple and direct democracy. The people of Athens decided, then and there, a specific proposal of the Council, or they might choose, after debate, to refer a different proposal to the Council, to be considered by it and proposed as a new motion at the next meeting of the Assembly.

Magistrates, Council and Assembly formed the framework of the government, but back of all lay the courts. These were really juries without a judge, for the presiding official was an archon who had no particular knowledge of the law. Nor did the jurors themselves have any special competence. In the place of case law or precedent the Athenians substituted a firm belief that every decision of a jury was a fresh reaffirmation of the general notion of what was right.

The jurors, like the councillors and magistrates (excepting the generals), were paid by the state. Altogether, when we add the soldiers and sailors, about 20,000 Athenians were on the payroll of their city. All this was made possible by the empire and its tribute, but when they finally disappeared, payment for public service became a very considerable burden. In the days of their greatest glory, however, the Athenians devised a democracy which gave them material as well as moral independence.

The violet-crowned city which Pericles led to empire and glory, to war and defeat, long vibrated with enthusiasm and confidence. For decades during the fifth century, the Athenians felt sure enough of themselves to permit a freedom of speech that often extended to biting self-criticism. Their love for their state, however, was tempered and controlled by a discipline that was imposed, not from above, but by each individual himself. This is clearly stated by Pericles in his immortal Funeral Oration, a statement of ideals, it should be added, rather than of rigid reality.

The terrible Peloponnesian War between Athens and Sparta, from which Greece never recovered, broke out in 431 B.C. At the end of the year's fighting, the people gathered, as was their custom, outside the city walls to listen to an oration especially prepared for the occasion. We must imagine ourselves in the beautiful cemetery, the Cerameicus, with the pink rock of the Acropolis and its marble temples to our backs. The profound contemporary Athenian historian, Thucydides the son of Olorus, describes the ceremony as follows:

> During the same winter, in accordance with an old national custom, the funeral of those who first fell in this war was celebrated by the Athenians at the public charge. The ceremony is as follows: Three days before the celebration they erect a tent in which the bones of the dead are laid out, and every

one brings to his own dead any offering which he pleases. At the time of the funeral the bones are placed in chests of cypress wood, which are conveyed on hearses; there is one chest for each tribe. They also carry a single empty litter decked with a pall for all whose bodies are missing, and cannot be recovered after the battle. The procession is accompanied by anyone who chooses, whether citizen or stranger, and the female relatives of the deceased are present at the place of interment and make lamentation. The public sepulcher is situated in the most beautiful spot outside the walls; there they always bury those who fall in war; only after the battle of Marathon the dead, in recognition of their pre-eminent valor, were interred on the field. When the remains have been laid in the earth, some man of known ability and high reputation, chosen by the city, delivers a suitable ora-tion over them; after which the people depart. Such is the manner of interment; and the ceremony was repeated from time to time throughout the war. Over those who were the first buried Pericles was chosen to speak. At the fitting moment he advanced from the sepulcher to a lofty stage, which had been erected in order that he might be heard as far as possible by the multitude, and spoke as follows:—

"Most of those who have spoken here before me have commended the lawgiver who added this oration to our other funeral customs; it seemed to them a worthy thing that such an honor should be given at their burial to the dead who have fallen on the field of battle. But I should have preferred that, when men's deeds have been brave, they should be honored in deed only, and with such an honor as this public funeral, which you are now witnessing. Then the reputation of many would not have been imperiled on the eloquence or want of eloquence of one, and their virtues believed or not as he spoke well or ill. For it is difficult to say neither too little nor too much; and even moderation is apt not to give the impression of truthfulness. The friend of the dead who knows the facts is likely to think that the words of the speaker fall short of his knowledge and of his wishes; another who is not so well informed, when he hears of anything which surpasses his own powers, will be envious and will suspect exaggeration. Mankind are tolerant of the praises of others so long as each hearer thinks that he can do as well or nearly as well himself, but, when the speaker rises above him, jealousy is aroused and he begins to be incredulous. However, since our ancestors have set the seal of their approval upon the practice, I must obey, and to the utmost of my power shall endeavor to satisfy the wishes and beliefs of all who hear me.

"I will speak first of our ancestors, for it is right and seemly that now, when we are lamenting the dead, a tribute should be paid to their memory. There has never been a time when they did not inhabit this land, which by their valor they have handed down from generation to generation, and we have received from them a free state. But if they were worthy of praise, still more were our fathers, who added to their inheritance, and after many a struggle transmitted to us their sons this great empire. And we ourselves assembled here today, who are still most of us in the vigor of life, have carried the work of improvement further, and have richly endowed our city with all things, so that she is sufficient for herself both in peace and war. Of the military exploits by which our various possessions were acquired, or of the energy with which we or our fathers drove back the tide of war, Hellenic or Barbarian, I will not speak; for the tale would be long and is familiar to you. But before

I praise the dead, I should like to point out by what principles of action we rose to power, and under what institutions and through what manner of life our empire became great. For I conceive that such thoughts are not unsuited to the occasion, and that this numerous assembly of citizens and strangers may profitably listen to them.

"Our form of government does not enter into rivalry with the institutions of others. We do not copy our neighbors, but are an example to them. It is true that we are called a democracy, for the administration is in the hands of the many and not of the few. But while the law secures equal justice to all alike in their private disputes, the claim of excellence is also recognized; and when a citizen is in any way distinguished, he is preferred to the public service, not as a matter of privilege, but as the reward of merit. Neither is poverty a bar, but a man may benefit his country whatever be the obscurity of his condition. There is no exclusiveness in our public life, and in our private intercourse we are not suspicious of one another, nor angry with our neighbor if he does what he likes; we do not put on sour looks at him which, though harmless, are not pleasant. While we are thus unconstrained in our private intercourse, a spirit of reverence pervades our public acts; we are prevented from doing wrong by respect for the authorities and for the laws, having an especial regard to those which are ordained for the protection of the injured as well as to those unwritten laws which bring upon the transgressor of them the reprobation of the general sentiment.

"And we have not forgotten to provide for our weary spirits many relaxations from toil; we have regular games and sacrifices throughout the year; our homes are beautiful and elegant; and the delight which we daily feel in all these things helps to banish melancholy. Because of the greatness of our city the fruits of the whole earth flow in upon us; so that we enjoy the goods of other countries as freely as of our own.

"Then, again, our military training is in many respects superior to that of our adversaries. Our city is thrown open to the world, and we never expel a foreigner or prevent him from seeing or learning anything of which the secret if revealed to an enemy might profit him. We rely not upon management or trickery, but upon our own hearts and hands. And in the matter of education, whereas they from early youth are always undergoing laborious exercises which are to make them brave, we live at ease, and yet are equally ready to face the perils which they face. And here is the proof. The Lacedæmonians come into Attica not by themselves, but with their whole confederacy following; we go alone into a neighbor's country; and although our opponents are fighting for their homes and we on a foreign soil, we have seldom any difficulty in overcoming them. Our enemies have never yet felt our united strength; the care of a navy divides our attention, and on land we are obliged to send our own citizens everywhere. But they, if they meet and defeat a part of our army, are as proud as if they had routed us all, and when defeated they pretend to have been vanquished by us all.

"If then we prefer to meet danger with a light heart but without laborious training, and with a courage which is gained by habit and not enforced by law, are we not greatly the gainers? Since we do not anticipate the pain, although, when the hour comes, we can be as brave as those who never allow themselves to rest; and thus too our city is equally admirable in peace and in war. For we are lovers of the beautiful, yet simple in our tastes, and we cultivate the mind without loss of manliness. Wealth we employ, not for talk and ostentation, but when there is a real use for it. To avow poverty with us is no disgrace; the true disgrace is in doing nothing to avoid it. An Athenian citizen does not neglect the state because he takes care of his own household; and even those of us who are engaged in business have a very fair idea of politics. We alone regard a man who takes no interest in public affairs, not as a harmless, but as a useless character; and if few of us are originators, we are all sound judges of a policy. The great impediment to action is, in our opinion, not discussion, but the want of that knowledge which is gained by discussion preparatory to action. For we have a peculiar power of thinking before we act and of acting too, whereas other men are courageous from ignorance but hesitate upon reflection. And they are surely to be esteemed the bravest spirits who, having the clearest sense both of the pains and pleasures of life, do not on that account shrink from danger. In doing good, again, we are unlike others; we make our friends by conferring, not by receiving favors. Now he who confers a favor is the firmer friend, because he would fain by kindness keep alive the memory of an obligation; but the recipient is colder in his feelings, because he knows that in requiting another's generosity he will not be winning gratitude but only paying a debt. We alone do good to our neighbors not upon a calculation of interest, but in the confidence of freedom and in a frank and fearless spirit. To sum up: I say that Athens is the school of Hellas, and that the individual Athenian in his own person seems to have the power of adapting himself to the most varied forms of action with the utmost versatility and grace. This is no passing and idle word, but truth and fact;

and the assertion is verified by the position to which these qualities have raised the state. For in the hour of trial Athens alone among her contemporaries is superior to the report of her. No enemy who comes against her is indignant at the reverses which he sustains at the hands of such a city; no subject complains that his masters are unworthy of him. And we shall assuredly not be without witnesses; there are mighty monuments of our power which will make us the wonder of this and of succeeding ages; we shall not need the praises of Homer or of any other panegyrist whose poetry may please for the moment, although his representation of the facts will not bear the light of day. For we have compelled every land and every sea to open a path for our valor, and have everywhere planted eternal memorials of our friendship and of our enmity. Such is the city for whose sake these men nobly fought and died; they could not bear the thought that she might be taken from them; and every one of us who survive should gladly toil on her behalf.

"I have dwelt upon the greatness of Athens because I want to show you that we are contending for a higher prize than those who enjoy none of these privileges, and to establish by manifest proof the merit of these men whom I am now commemorating. Their loftiest praise has been already spoken. For in magnifying the city I have magnified them, and men like them whose virtues made her glorious. And of how few Hellenes can it be said as of them, that their deeds when weighed in the balance have been found equal to their fame! Methinks that a death such as theirs has been given the true measure of a man's worth; it may be the first revelation of his virtues, but is at any rate their final seal. For even those who come short in other ways may justly plead the valor

with which they have fought for their country; they
have blotted out the evil with the good, and have
benefited the state more by their public services than
they have injured her by their private actions. None
of these men were enervated by wealth or hesitated
to resign the pleasures of life; none of them put off
the evil day in the hope, natural to poverty, that a
man, though poor, may one day become rich. But,
deeming that the punishment of their enemies was
sweeter than any of these things, and that they could
fall in no nobler cause, they determined at the hazard
of their lives to be honorably avenged, and to leave
the rest. They resigned to hope their unknown chance
of happiness; but in the face of death they resolved
to rely upon themselves alone. And when the moment
came they were minded to resist and suffer, rather
than to fly and save their lives; they ran away from
the word of dishonor, but on the battlefield their feet
stood fast, and in an instant, at the height of their
fortune, they passed away from the scene, not of their
fear, but of their glory.

"Such was the end of these men; they were worthy
of Athens, and the living need not desire to have a
more heroic spirit, although they may pray for a less
fatal issue. The value of such a spirit is not to be
expressed in words. Any one can discourse to you for
ever about the advantages of a brave defense, which
you know already. But instead of listening to him
I would have you day by day fix your eyes upon the
greatness of Athens, until you become filled with the
love of her; and when you are impressed by the spectacle of her glory, reflect that this empire has been
acquired by men who knew their duty and had the
courage to do it, who in the hour of conflict had the
fear of dishonor always present to them, and who,
if ever they failed in an enterprise, would not allow

their virtues to be lost to their country, but freely gave their lives to her as the fairest offering which they could present at her feast. The sacrifice which they collectively made was individually repaid to them; for they received again each one for himself a praise which grows not old, and the noblest of all sepulchers—I speak not of that in which their remains are laid, but of that in which their glory survives, and is proclaimed always and on every fitting occasion both in word and deed. For the whole earth is the sepulcher of famous men; not only are they commemorated by columns and inscriptions in their own country, but in foreign lands there dwells also an unwritten memorial of them, graven not on stone but in the hearts of men. Make them your examples, and, esteeming courage to be freedom and freedom to be happiness, do not weigh too nicely the perils of war. The unfortunate who has no hope of a change for the better has less reason to throw away his life than the prosperous who, if he survive, is always liable to a change for the worse, and to whom any accidental fall makes the most serious difference. To a man of spirit, cowardice and disaster coming together are far more bitter than death striking him unperceived at a time when he is full of courage and animated by the general hope.

"Wherefore I do not now commiserate the parents of the dead who stand here; I would rather comfort them. You know that your life has been passed amid manifold vicissitudes; and that they may be deemed fortunate who have gained most honor, whether an honorable death like theirs, or an honorable sorrow like yours, and whose days have been so ordered that the term of their happiness is likewise the term of their life. I know how hard it is to make you feel this, when the good fortune of others will too often remind you of the gladness which once lightened your hearts. And sorrow is felt at the want of those blessings, not which a man never knew, but which were a part of his life before they were taken from him. Some of you are of an age at which they may hope to have other children, and they ought to bear their sorrow better; not only will the children who may hereafter be born make them forget their own lost ones, but the city will be doubly a gainer. She will not be left desolate, and she will be safer. For a man's counsel cannot have equal weight or worth, when he alone has no children to risk in the general danger. To those of you who have passed their prime, I say: 'Congratulate yourselves that you have been happy during the greater part of your days; remember that your life of sorrow will not last long, and be comforted by the glory of those who are gone. For the love of honor alone is ever young, and not riches, as some say, but honor is the delight of men when they are old and useless.'

"To you who are the sons and brothers of the departed, I see that the struggle to emulate them will be an arduous one. For all men praise the dead, and, however pre-eminent your virtue may be, hardly will you be thought, I do not say to equal, but even to approach them. The living have their rivals and detractors, but when a man is out of the way, the honor and good will which he receives is unalloyed. And, if I am to speak of womanly virtues to those of you who will henceforth be widows, let me sum them up in one short admonition: To a woman not to show more weakness than is natural to her sex is a great glory, and not to be talked about for good or for evil among men.

"I have paid the required tribute, in obedience to the law, making use of such fitting words as I had.

The tribute of deeds has been paid in part; for the dead have been honorably interred, and it remains only that their children should be maintained at the public charge until they are grown up: this is the solid prize with which, as with a garland, Athens crowns her sons living and dead, after a struggle like theirs. For where the rewards of virtue are greatest, there the noblest citizens are enlisted in the service of the state. And now, when you have duly lamented, every one his own dead, you may depart."

We are fortunate to possess this moving and very precious description of a great democracy caught up in mortal conflict. Of course, the patriotism and high ideals on which Pericles insisted demanded far too much of the ordinary man and could not last long. When Pericles himself died not much later, the descent of the Athenians to a more familiar plane was rapid and decisive.

The ideals and love of city never wholly died, however. In the crisis of the long war, which ended with Athens' defeat in 404 B.C., political offenders might, and occasionally did, lose their civic rights, but it is stirring to reflect that, in the year before the final defeat, the comic poet Aristophanes appealed to his fellow Athenians to restore these rights. His play, *The Frogs,* so touched the audience that it was accorded the unique honor of a second presentation a short time later.

It was also at the end of the war that another poet, the tragedian Sophocles, wrote his *Œdipus at Colonus.* Sophocles was in his ninetieth year, and the play was produced posthumously after the cessation of hostilities. There is an ode within the play that celebrates Sophocles' birthplace, Colonus, a suburb of Athens, and Attica, the district of which Athens was the capital. We imagine the chorus turning and counterturning—the strophe and antistrophe of the chorus, as it is called—while it sang brightly during days that must have seemed very dark indeed:

Strophe 1
CHORUS: *Of all the land far famed for goodly steeds,*
Thou com'st, O stranger, to the noblest spot,
    Colonus, glistening bright,
Where evermore, in thickets freshly green,
    The clear-voiced nightingale
    Still haunts, and pours her song,
    By purpling ivy hid,
And the thick leafage sacred to the God,
    With all its myriad fruits.
    By mortal's foot untouched,
    By sun's hot ray unscathed,
    Sheltered from every blast;
There wanders Dionysus evermore,
    In full, wild revelry,
And waits upon the Nymphs who nursed his youth.

Antistrophe 1
And there, beneath the gentle dews of heaven,
The fair narcissus with its clustered bells
    Blooms ever, day by day,
Of old the wreath of mightiest Goddesses;
    And crocus golden-eyed;
    And still unslumbering flow
    Cephisus' wandering streams;
They fail not from their spring, but evermore,
    Swift-rushing into birth,
    Over the plain they sweep,
    The land of broad, full breast,
    With clear and stainless wave:

49

Nor do the Muses in their minstrel choirs,
  Hold it in slight esteem,
Nor Aphrodite with her golden reins.

Strophe 2
And in it grows a marvel such as ne'er
  On Asia's soil I heard,
Nor the great Dorian isle from Pelops named,
    A plant self-sown, that knows
    No touch of withering age,
    Terror of hostile swords,
    Which here on this our ground
    Its high perfection gains,
The grey-green foliage of the olive-tree,
    Rearing a goodly race:
    And never more shall man,
    Or young, or bowed with years,
    Give forth the fierce command,
    And lay it low in dust.
    For lo! the eye of Zeus,
    Zeus of our olive groves,
    That sees eternally,
    Casteth its glance thereon,
And she, Athena, with the clear, grey eyes.

Antistrophe 2
And yet another praise is mine to sing,
  Gift of the mighty God
To this our city, mother of us all,
    Her greatest, noblest boast,
    Famed for her goodly steeds,
    Famed for her bounding colts,
    Famed for her sparkling sea.
Poseidon, son of Cronus, Lord and King,
    To Thee this boast we owe,
    For first in these our streets

Thou to the untamed horse
Did'st use the conquering bit:
And here the well-shaped oar,
By skilled hands deftly plied,
Still leapeth through the sea,
Following in wondrous guise,
The fair Nereids with their hundred feet.

The poet who wrote these lines typified, perhaps better than anyone, the Greek ideal. In the year 443 B.C., for example, Sophocles was appointed by Pericles chief treasurer during a reorganization of the Athenian Empire, and three years later, having meanwhile produced the *Antigone,* he was a general under Pericles in the Samian War.

It was a world that respected men of action: the way to get an education was by living fully in the present, not in a relatively unimportant past. As Thucydides himself says at the outset of his *History,* "Judging from the evidence which I am able to trust after most careful inquiry, I should imagine that former ages were not great either in their wars or in anything else."

The Greeks, and pre-eminently the Athenians, whose city became "the teacher of Hellas," placed intellectual inquiry high among the things that really counted in life. As a result, they asked practically every great question that has ever engaged mankind: the advantages of wealth; the nature of the gods and the immortality of the soul; the true character of democracy; the meaning of justice and tyranny, cruelty, beauty, and love. Athens in the fifth century B.C. very obviously did not answer these questions with a finality, nor always with marked success, but some of her best minds made a noble attempt, and it is by its best minds that any civilization may fairly ask to be judged.

IV

ART AND THOUGHT

A CENTURIES-LONG evolution in both architecture and sculpture culminated in the Parthenon. It was never surpassed in antiquity, for the entire Greek experience went into its creation and, as generally happens when the pinnacle of an art has been reached, a new mental standpoint was necessary for further significant growth. This required in turn, if not a new attitude toward the world on the part of the people as a whole, at the very least a sustained eagerness to experiment. The Greeks did not have this—perhaps the Peloponnesian War made it impossible—so that, within two decades of the Parthenon's completion, Greek architecture takes on an interest that is largely historical, intense and even romantic though that may be.

Greek art, like Greek literature, was influenced by both religion and politics. It would be idle to attempt a statement of the typical Greek's religious beliefs, for they ran all the way from superstition to atheism. The doctrine of sin and the need to purify oneself by washing in blood were as present as the attachment to magic and the worship of ghosts. In sharp contrast stood the monotheism of the intellectual, such as Æschylus, who prayed to "Zeus, whoe'er he be."

Nevertheless, the religion of the Olympian gods was the common inheritance of all Greeks and in varying degree held their allegiance. The general picture of the gods had been set by Homer, who placed the chief ones on Mt. Olympus, where they lived forever under the presidency of Zeus, the father of gods and men. They quarreled among themselves, debated the destinies of men, and lived a life of ease with all the virtues and faults of mankind. It was easy to feel close to such gods and to imagine, when anger or love or some other emotion seized you, that an actual god had taken possession of you.

No priestly class was necessary for the worship of these gods, and such priests as there were were officials chosen annually for routine tasks. The individual sacrificed and prayed directly to the gods. He might consult an oracle, as that of Apollo at Delphi, but usually this had to do with the need for advice on some homely subject.

Since the Greeks worshiped gods who were at once human and divine, it seems almost inevitable that their first statues should have attempted a general impression of mankind. The sculptors hoped to portray the type, the generic, rather than the particular and individual, or, if we may use a cliché, they were more interested in Man than men. There is, accordingly, an aloofness or other-worldly quality to early Greek sculpture, something which is akin to both the human and the divine.

At the beginning, the sculptor could not handle his tools and materials easily, and the finished product was far from realistic. The ears might be too far back, the lips might not come together naturally. To compensate for his lack of technical skill, the sculptor stylized his figure. A decorative stomach, perhaps diamond in shape, took the place of musculature. More important still was the sculptor's active determination to achieve naturalism, for it made him breathe into his stone or bronze a wonderfully exuberant and vital elasticity and strength. His statues fairly burst with life and energy.

There is no doubt whatever about the Greek sculptor's desire to gain naturalism, for we can study his product decade by decade and see when the tear duct and other anatomical features first appear. The whole progress of Greek sculpture was toward ever greater realism. It was merely one side of a highly rational people and kept step with their increasing belief in the dignity of man. By the fifth century, growing individualism, a firm belief at Athens in democracy, and the introduction of new religious cults, especially mystical ones from Thrace and the East, weakened the hold of the hereditary gods on educated and uneducated alike. This new attitude toward life, combined with great technical proficiency and an extraordinarily exact perception of the human form, produced idealized statues where it is often quite impossible to say whether gods or men are represented.

The architectural tradition back of the Parthenon was fully as long as the sculptural. The temple was the most important of Greek buildings, and the chief characteristic of it is the rows of columns. Hence arose two special problems, long in the solving. The columns and the courses above them—the so-called entablature—stood upon a platform, which was approached by three steps. A straight, level platform, however, unfortunately appears to dip in the center. In order to correct this optical illusion and give the impression that the building is not ready to fall down—that it is full of life—Greek architects learned to curve the platform and make it rise from each corner toward the center.

The other special problem was presented by the columns, which in their long rows may appear rigid and even likely to break under the weight imposed upon them. The architects got around the rigidity by not placing the columns vertically, but allowing them to lean both backward and toward the center of the line. As for the weight—presented by the entablature of architrave and frieze, the cornice and roof—we surely might fear that eventually the tapering column would break into pieces. Consequently, the architects gave a slight convex curve, known as entasis, to the column; it appears as a gentle, elastic swelling in the central sweep of the column, as if to suggest that the great weight above had already come down and that the column had comfortably yielded to it in advance.

The primary purpose of the capital, or crowning feature of the shaft, was functional, as was the case with everything in Greek architecture, until repetition killed originality. Its chief purpose, that is to say, was to provide a broader base on which to rest the entablature than the shaft itself allowed. That accomplished, the Greeks turned to its refinement, to its secondary purpose, which was to provide a transition for the eye from the vertical line of the column to the horizontal of the entablature. The first member of the capital—a convex molding, for it is neither vertical nor horizontal, called the echinus—interrupts the upward flight of the eye, which has been accentuated by the fluting of the shaft. On top of the echinus, and part of the same block, is the second member of the capital, a small horizontal slab known architecturally as the abacus. Now we are ready for the horizontal lines of the entablature.

It took the Greek architects long to solve these problems satisfactorily, and their earlier attempts are often quite painful to the eye. In their own way, moreover, the architects were themselves restricted by convention, for the origins of the Doric order of architecture were in wooden construction. (The Parthenon is of the Doric order, the other two orders being the Ionic and Corinthian.) Consequently, when the Greeks were able to build in stone, they carried over certain details which made sense only in wood. This is immediately clear when we look at the six little drops, "guttæ," which occur at regular intervals along the top of the architrave (the first level range or course above the columns), for originally they were wooden nails, driven into the beam ends which rested on the architrave. Or consider the next course above, the frieze of triglyphs and metopes. Originally the triglyphs—vertical channels that project—had been designed to protect from the weather the wooden beam ends directly behind them. And the metopes—sunk panels between the triglyphs and often sculptured, hence the course is called the frieze—had the duty of keeping the rain and wind from blowing in between the beams.

The Parthenon is the most wonderful example of these and other details and refinements. It was begun in 447 B. C., just as soon as Pericles persuaded the Athenians to reimpose the tribute on their allies. As general artistic supervisor of new buildings he appointed Pheidias, who also was the chief sculptor. So much sculpture was carved, however, that we cannot say whether a particular piece was done by Pheidias or an associate. The one thing certain about the sculpture of the Parthenon is that great care was taken with the overall plan, as well as the execution.

The Parthenon was sacred to Athena Parthenos—Athena the Virgin—the protecting deity of the state and patron of arts and sciences, the symbol of truth and wisdom. It dominates the Acropolis and contributes to an extraordinary color effect, for it is made of a marble, from nearby Mt. Pentelicus, that contains a conspicuous amount of iron. The iron streaks come out as a golden glow against the predominant white. We must imagine the Parthenon standing on the pink living rock of the Acropolis, with a bright sun and blue sky overhead. At our feet is the city, now as in the past stretching out into the Attic Plain, which has always been filled with olive groves. On three sides the plain is rimmed by mountains—Parnes, Pentelicus, Hymettus, famous for its honey—which turn with the brilliance of the sun from russet to purple. On the fourth side, not five miles distant, lies Homer's wine-dark sea, though to our eyes it seems to be more of a peacock blue. Beyond the islands lie the mountains of the Peloponnesus, long, sharp mountain ranges, as they are in Greece, and doubtless contributing to the sharpness of Greek thinking.

The architects of the Parthenon, Ictinus and Callicrates, laid out a building that was larger than usual—228 feet long, 101 feet wide, and 65 feet high—with eight columns front and rear, and seventeen along the sides. An extraordinary feature, illustrating the fact that all ideas were at home in Athens, was the incorporation of Ionic details into the Doric structure. The grace and delicacy of the Ionic order contrast with the majesty of the Doric, and to combine them in the same building was as bold and daring a step as it was practically unique.

The chief, and certainly the most famous and beautiful, Ionic feature was the continuous frieze that ran round the top of the wall enclosing the chambers or cellas. Since the Ionic frieze course, unlike the Doric, has no triglyphs, it was possible for Pheidias to carve a continuous procession in relief. The scene represents the Panathenaic procession, a mid-summer festival, when the best young blood of Athens, youths on horseback and afoot, girls with offerings, brought a new robe for the old wooden statue of Athena on the Acropolis. At the east end of the Parthenon, over the main entrance, are gathered the gods of Olympus, giving their blessing to this purely local celebration. The whole frieze extended more than 520 feet on blocks about 40 inches high and is actually a grand example of drawing in stone.

Pheidias, however, was confronted by a very real problem, since a ceiling projected from the top of the cella wall to the colonnade. This meant that the Ionic frieze was in the shade, and such reflected light as came from below would cast shadows upward, obscuring the faces of the figures. Accordingly, the whole frieze was carved in very low relief, the lower parts of the figures especially so.

The triangular gables or pediments, above the columns at either end, were filled with sculptures in the round. The east pediment brings us to Mt. Olympus, where Athena has just sprung fully armed from the head of Zeus. Gods and goddesses stand marveling at the wondrous birth, while toward the corners of the pediment, other deities, not yet aware of the news, watch the rising sun and setting moon. The celebration of the birth of Athens' goddess takes on cosmic significance, which is repeated in the west pediment, where Athena and Poseidon strive to be selected by the Athenians as their patron.

These sculptures—together with the carved metopes on the outside and no doubt, though it has long since disappeared, the gold and ivory statue of Athena within the main cella—show how wonderfully adjusted to his world the Greek was. A world of injustice and war, of poverty and illness, it certainly was, but in the Parthenon we catch no glimpse of this. Instead, we have an idealization of man, sure of himself, confident that he can surmount his difficulties and mold the future to his desires. Could any greater proof be found than in the so-called Dionysus of the east pediment, does it not speak directly to us, with no need of an interpreter? And is it not an interesting sidelight on the Greek spirit that the Parthenon may be described as a political spectacle as easily as a religious monument?

Although work on the Parthenon was to continue for six more years, its formal dedication in 438 B.C. was seized upon by Pericles as an auspicious moment to commence new gateways to the Acropolis. Unfortunately, the outbreak of the Peloponnesian War in 431 B.C. prevented the completion of the Propylæa, but it is a tribute to the resilience of the Athenians that a decade later—during the first lull in the war, known as the Peace of Nicias— they immediately turned their thoughts to the construction of another temple. This was the delicate Temple of Athena Nike (Victory), perched on a bastion before the Propylæa.

Still more extraordinary, however, and indeed almost incredible, is the fact that, as the war continued, bringing with it unparalleled atrocities and suffering, the Athenians were able to build the Erechtheum, their most elaborate temple. The rich decoration and finely carved details—such as the bases and capitals of columns, and the honeysuckle ornamentation along the top of the cella— blend marvelously with the delicate grace of the Ionic order of architecture. The Erechtheum has two porches, one on the north with a beautifully carved door, and the other on the south, where stately Maidens, or Caryatids, hold up the roof.

The tribute of their empire made it easier, of course, for the Athenians to erect these and other buildings. If we disregard the interests of their allies, as the Athenians themselves often did, if we overlook the policies of Pericles that led squarely into the war which was to change the character of Greece forever, we cannot deny that at least the Athenians provided richly for their own full and active participation in the business of living. The imperial trib- ute, as we have already remarked, also made possible pay- ment for jury and other public service and very particu- larly it enabled the people to take part in festivals to a degree that would have astounded an earlier generation.

Of all the festivals, the most important by far was the City Dionysia. This was held during the spring in honor of Dionysus, god of fertility and patron of the theater. As with the art, a religious atmosphere pervaded the cele- bration and, as with the art again, state support meant a certain public control and direction of the occasion. It was altogether fitting, the Athenians believed, to mix politics and religion with art and literature, indeed to join together into a component pattern all the manifold aspects of life. Moreover, in the case of the dramatic pro- ductions, a keen competitive spirit heightened the excite- ment. This, too, was typically Greek.

For example, the tragic and comic poets, who wished to be represented at the time of the City Dionysia, were invited to submit their plays to a committee well in ad- vance of the celebration. Three tragic and five comic poets were ultimately chosen. Each dramatist oversaw his own production, but since a chorus (in the case of tragedy) numbered fifteen amateurs who could hardly spare the time for rehearsal, a wealthy citizen, known as a *choregos,* was assigned to each playwright to cover expenses. This was one of several forms of direct taxation which the Athenians imposed upon the rich, but it was not resented, for the *choregos* who was fortunate enough to support a winning play had the privilege of erecting at his own expense a monument in honor of the fact.

The actors were professionals and were paid by the state. Since each tragedy had only three actors (though, if necessary, an actor might take more than one role), it would have been manifestly unfair for a dramatist to secure the services of the three best actors. Accordingly, each was assigned his leading actor, or protagonist, and again, at the end of the festival, a prize was awarded the best protagonist, and his name, together with those of the dramatist and winning play, were inscribed on stone.

The scene of the festival was the Theater of Dionysus, an open-air structure on the south slope of the Athenian Acropolis. The auditorium seated approximately eighteen thousand persons. At its foot was a level, circular area, called the orchestra, where the action took place. No matter what their role, the actors (as well as the members of the chorus) were men, who wore masks designed to set the general type of the character they portrayed, for in a theater of this size facial expressions and other nuances of acting would be lost. No doubt the masks also made it easier for the actors to be heard, though the acoustics of Greek theaters is excellent.

In the middle of the orchestra stood the thymele, an altar sacred to Dionysus and garlanded for the occasion. On its steps sat musicians, for there was much singing and dancing in a Greek play. Across the orchestra from the auditorium rose the scene building, which served as a simple background for the production.

The City Dionysia occupied six days, six long and

happy, albeit serious, days. The first day was ordinarily given over to a great procession, the second to a competition between ten dithyrambic choruses of fifty each. On the third day five comedies, each by a different dramatist, were presented. The final three days belonged to tragedy. On each of these days a different playwright presented a group of three plays, often on the same general theme and known as a trilogy. Of all the trilogies produced in ancient Greece, only one (the *Oresteia* of Æschylus) is extant. It is not generally known how tremendous our losses are, but it is a fact that only forty-seven plays survive from the thousands which were originally written.

The Greek tragic poets went back into the legendary past to find their themes, but they so handled them, especially by insisting on human values, that they gave them a universal and eternal quality. The gods, for example, appear in their plays and create a religious atmosphere, such as the Dionysiac festival itself provided, but the primary appeal of a Greek tragedy is to the intellect and not the emotions. Aristotle placed the primary emphasis on the emotional, but he lived in the century after the great Athenian dramatists and did not always understand fifth-century standards.

Æschylus, the first of the three great Athenian tragic poets, concerned himself in *Prometheus Bound* with the problem of evil and asked why it should exist. How can God let man suffer? This is exactly the same question that his younger contemporary, Sophocles, asks in the *Philoctetes*, where the conflict between patriotism and conscience is raised. Why, asks Sophocles, are good men made to suffer? Job, too, asked this question.

Æschylus was a deeply religious man as well as a master of language and imagery. In his *Oresteia*—the trilogy

composed of *Agamemnon, Choëphoræ,* and *Eumenides*
—we observe how a succession of curses falls upon the
House of Atreus, until finally mercy is joined to justice
and man learns that obedience and wisdom come from
suffering. Æschylus was at heart both poet and teacher,
and though the dramatists after him were not conspicuously didactic, the drama inevitably spread advanced ideas
throughout the body politic.

How could it have been otherwise, when we recall that
during the City Dionysia alone the Athenians for several
concentrated days were transported to the level of universal tragedy and gave themselves over completely to the
most serious of themes?

Aristotle points out in his *Poetics* that tragedy is an
"imitation" of an action that is serious, complete, and of
a certain magnitude. Its function is to rouse pity and fear
in the audience and thus to provide a *catharsis,* or purg-
ing, of these and similar emotions. The ideal tragic hero,
he continues, is a highly renowned man, though not a pre-
eminently virtuous one, whose misfortune is brought
upon him by some error of judgment or frailty, rather
than by vice and depravity.

It was in Sophocles' Theban Saga—three plays, *Œdipus
the King Œdipus at Colonus,* and *Antigone,* which deal
with the ancient city of Thebes, though they were written
at widely different times—and more particularly in the
person of Œdipus himself that Aristotle found the illustration of his famous definition. The situation of Œdipus,
who has unwittingly murdered his father and married his
mother, is so utterly tragic that our own minds are finally
purged of the pity and fear which he arouses in us. We
are moved by man's dignity in the face of forces greater
than himself and by his endurance under stress. Though

his mental anguish is hardly bearable, Œdipus does not plead ignorance, but accepts responsibility for his acts. An heroic grandeur gradually envelops him until finally at Colonus, Sophocles' own birthplace in Attica, he leaves this life in the grandest scene achieved by paganism. The main problem of the *Antigone,* on the other hand, is reminiscent of that raised by the *Philoctetes,* for it concerns the conflict of duty; specifically, does God's law take precedence over man's?

Although Sophocles casts in universal terms his preoccupation with the effect of life upon the development of character, the manner of his treatment is outstandingly Hellenic. This was not true of Euripides, who in his iconoclasm heralds a new and modern day. It is easy to appreciate that during his lifetime Euripides would be disliked for his advanced views and receive first prize on only four occasions, though after his death he was the most popular of the Athenian dramatists. Few people have preached on occasion more insistently that the individual is responsible for his conduct. A skeptic and realist, his sympathies went out to the downtrodden and oppressed.

This is particularly true of *The Trojan Women,* where Euripides paints the horrors awaiting the women of a conquered city, and yet it was only part of a larger theme. In the year before its production, the Athenians had committed one of the worst outrages of the Peloponnesian War, an unprovoked attack upon the neutral island of Melos and had killed the men and enslaved the women and children. Preparations for another imperialistic folly, the expedition against Sicily, began immediately. In the midst of all this, Euripides dared speak out and in *The Trojan Women* told his fellow Athenians that war is not only cruel and useless but harms the victors as much as the vanquished. It took courage to do this—if we may judge by the silences of other days—but such was the atmosphere of Athens that Euripides did not stand alone. Not only did Aristophanes advocate peace in several plays, but in his *History of the Peloponnesian War* Thucydides selected the same Melian episode to illustrate to what depths a once humane state could fall.

An acute and profound student of human nature, Euripides asks in *The Bacchæ* whether man can live by reason alone. Must not moderation and restraint apply to rationalism no less than to emotionalism? This was implicit in Delphi's famous precept, "Nothing to excess," and appears again in the *Hippolytus,* where an excessive devotion to chastity brings destruction. It is part, though only part, of the theme of the *Medea,* where a woman, who has the power to do as she wishes, acts with none of the restraints that civilization imposes. But here Euripides has a larger target—the smugness and provincialism of the Greek himself, who divided the world into a handful of Greeks and myriads of barbarians. Medea is a terrible woman, quite true; moreover, it is outrageous of her, a non-Greek, to imagine that she could marry a Greek. But consider, says Euripides, all that she did for Jason, how she gave up home and family for him, only to be shabbily treated by a cad.

Greek tragedy was compounded of diverse primitive elements. So, too, the origin of comedy lay in the dim past, in a fertility rite, which explains in part the bawdiness of Aristophanes, the greatest of Athenian comic poets, though it is difficult to believe that there was anything he loved more. The comedy of situation, which is essentially our form of comedy, was to develop later, but in Aristophanes' time the aim of the playwright was to examine the issues of the day and to attack living persons, who as likely as not were seated in the theater. The complete freedom of speech at Athens seemed to go hand in hand with a carefree lack of modesty, with an optimistic faith in the power of a dynamic society.

Of course, the first purpose of Aristophanes was to amuse and entertain, but since there is no better way of deflating an enemy than to make him a laughingstock, the comic poet was able to impress his views on the audience and advance the interests of his class. As a landowner whose farms were overrun by the Spartans each year, Aristophanes opposed the Peloponnesian War and particularly in the *Lysistrata* proposed a very effective, though highly fantastic, way of bringing it to an end. As a conservative, he disliked the new thought and attacked Euripides in *The Frogs* and Socrates so vigorously in *The Clouds* that this play permanently prejudiced the Athenians against him.

When we turn to the historical Socrates, it seems quite extraordinary that the Athenians could ever have allowed themselves to put him to death, no matter how false the charges. But it was a new day, and Greek civilization had suddenly become tired. Five years earlier, Athens had fallen to Sparta, her empire had disappeared and, even for a time, her democracy. Though great men lived in the next century, such as Plato, Aristotle, and Praxiteles, the individual felt lost in the complex and changing world, and it was not until near the end of the century that Alexander was able to give a new direction to the Greek spirit.

Still, in their heyday and for seventy years of his life, the Athenians felt strong enough of themselves to listen to Socrates. Some of them, such as the young Plato, were awakened to lives of intense intellectual activity. Socrates was a true child of Athenian democracy. In the previous century, especially in Ionia in Asia Minor, Greek thinkers had concerned themselves with an inquiry into nature, but they lacked the scientific instruments to carry it very far. Now, in the new day of democracy with its theory of human equality, they turned to the study of man. The shift of emphasis from the world to man led to individualism and a critical appraisal of the old answers to the problems of life. Tradition, so the poets and others held, no longer sufficed as a guide.

Instructors in wisdom, known as sophists, began by giving men all the knowledge they needed, presumably, to become statesmen, the royal road to power. But they split hairs so nicely and were so impudent in their manner that they filled many people with disgust. The mass mind, however, is notoriously incapable of making fine distinctions, and accordingly, when Aristophanes portrayed Socrates as the leading sophist of the day, there were few to find fault with him.

Socrates charged no fee for instruction nor was he in any other sense a sophist. He gave his life to preparing young men to serve their state in war and peace to the limit of their intellectual, physical, and spiritual power. A poor man himself, he had had little time or opportunity for study. He performed his duties as soldier and Councillor and faithfully sacrificed to the gods of the state, but most of his time he spent in thought and discussion. He loved to go where people congregated, and though he claimed no knowledge himself, it was easy for him as the most redoubtable thinker of his time to prove a person ignorant of the topic under discussion.

In his conversations with friends and strangers, Socrates

sought by induction to establish definitions of general terms—what, for example, do we mean by piety, by the beautiful and ugly, nobility and cowardice, a state, democracy? He held that the argument of design proved the existence of God, that man was made by God and the world, therefore, for man. It followed that the best of institutions are the most God-fearing. In a sense, he created a body of ethical science for men to follow. "There are two things," Aristotle declared, "that one would rightly attribute to Socrates: inductive reasoning and universal definition."

Is there a more eternal question than the need of communicating immortality to our human natures? Socrates, or at any rate his famous pupil Plato, thought not, and in *The Symposium* Plato puts these words into Socrates' mouth:

"At present let me endeavor, to the best of my power, to repeat to you, on the basis of the points which have been agreed upon between me and Agathon, a discourse concerning Love, which I formerly heard from the prophetess Diotima, who was profoundly skilled in this and many other doctrines, and who, ten years before the plague, procured to the Athenians, through their sacrifices, a delay of the disease; for it was she who taught me the science of things relating to Love.

"As you well remarked, Agathon, we ought to declare who and what is Love, and then his works. It is easiest to relate them in the same order as the foreign prophetess observed when, questioning me, she related them. For I said to her much the same things that Agathon has just said to me—that Love was a great deity, and that he was beautiful; and she refuted me with the same reasons as I have employed to refute Agathon, compelling me to infer that he was neither beautiful nor good, as I said.—'What then,' I objected, 'O Diotima, is Love ugly and evil?'—'Good words, I entreat you,' said Diotima; 'do you think that everything which is not beautiful, must of necessity be ugly?'—'Certainly.'—'And everything that is not wise, ignorant? Do you not perceive that there is something between ignorance and wisdom?'— 'What is that?'—'To have a right opinion or conjecture. Observe, that this kind of opinion, for which no reason can be rendered, cannot be called knowledge; for how can that be called knowledge, which is without evidence or reason? Nor ignorance, on the other hand; for how can that be called ignorance which arrives at the persuasion of that which it really is? A right opinion is something between understanding and ignorance.'—I confessed that what she alleged was true.—'Do not then say,' she continued, 'that what is not beautiful is of necessity deformed, nor what is not good is of necessity evil; nor, since you have confessed that Love is neither beautiful nor good, infer, therefore, that he is deformed or evil, but rather something intermediate.'

" 'But,' I said, 'love is confessed by all to be a great God.'—'Do you mean, when you say all, all those who know, or those who know not, what they say?'—'All collectively.'—'And how can that be, Socrates?' said she laughing; 'how can he be acknowledged to be a great God, by those who assert that he is not even a God at all?'—'And who are they?' I said—'You for one, and I for another.'—'How can you say that, Diotima?'—'Easily,' she replied, 'and with truth; for tell me, do you not own that all the Gods are beautiful and happy? or will you presume to maintain that any God is otherwise?'—'By Zeus, not I!'—'Do you not call those alone happy who possess all things that are beautiful and good?'—'Certainly.'—'You have confessed that Love, through his desire for things beautiful and good, possesses not those materials of happiness.'—'Indeed such was my concession.'—'But how can we conceive a God to be without the possession of what is beautiful and good?'—'In no manner, I confess.'—'Observe, then, that you do not consider Love to be a God.'—'What, then,' I said, 'is Love a mortal?'—'By no means.'—'But what, then?'—'Like those things which I have before instanced he is neither mortal nor immortal, but something intermediate.'—'What is that, O Diotima?'—'A great dæmon, Socrates; and everything dæmoniacal holds an intermediate place between what is divine and what is mortal.'

" 'What is his power and nature?' I inquired.—'He interprets and makes a communication between divine and human things, conveying the prayers and sacrifices of men to the Gods, and communicating the commands and directions concerning the mode of worship most pleasing to them, from Gods to men. He fills up that intermediate space between these two classes of beings, so as to bind together, by his own power, the whole universe of things. Through him subsist all divination, and the science of sacred things as it relates to sacrifices, and expiations, and disenchantments, and prophecy, and magic. The divine nature cannot immediately communicate with what is human, but all that intercourse and converse which is conceded by the Gods to men, both whilst they sleep and when they wake, subsists through the intervention of Love; and he who is wise in the science of this intercourse is supremely happy, and participates in the dæmoniacal nature; whilst he who is wise in any other science or art, remains a mere ordinary slave.

These dæmons are, indeed, many and various, and one of them is Love.'

" 'Who are the parents of Love?' I inquired.—'The history of what you ask,' replied Diotima, 'is somewhat long; nevertheless I will explain it to you. On the birth of Aphrodite the Gods celebrated a great feast, and among them came Plenty, the son of Metis. After supper, Poverty, observing the profusion, came to beg, and stood beside the door. Plenty being drunk with nectar, for wine was not yet invented, went out into Zeus' garden, and fell into a deep sleep. Poverty wishing to have a child by Plenty, on account of her low estate, lay down by him, and from his embraces conceived Love. Love is, therefore, the follower and servant of Aphrodite, because he was conceived at her birth, and because by nature he is a lover of all that is beautiful, and Aphrodite was beautiful. And since Love is the child of Poverty and Plenty, his nature and fortune participate in that of his parents. He is forever poor, and so far from being delicate and beautiful, as mankind imagine, he is squalid and withered; he flies low along the ground, and is homeless and unsandalled; he sleeps without covering before the doors, and in the unsheltered streets; possessing thus far his mother's nature, that he is ever the companion of want. But, inasmuch as he participates in that of his father, he is forever scheming to obtain things which are good and beautiful; he is fearless, vehement, and strong; a dreadful hunter, forever weaving some new contrivance; exceedingly cautious and prudent, and full of resources; he is also, during his whole existence, a philosopher, a powerful enchanter, a wizard, and a subtle sophist. And, as his nature is neither mortal nor immortal, on the same day when he is fortunate and successful, he will at one time flourish, and then die away, and then, according to his father's na-

ture, again revive. All that he acquires perpetually
flows away from him, so that Love is never either rich
or poor, and holding forever an intermediate state between ignorance and wisdom. The case stands thus;—
no God philosophizes or desires to become wise, for
he is wise; nor, if there exist any other being who is
wise, does he philosophize. Nor do the ignorant philosophize, for they desire not to become wise; for this
is the evil of ignorance, that he who has neither intelligence, nor virtue, nor delicacy of sentiment, im-
agines that he possesses all those things sufficiently.
He seeks not, therefore, that possession, of whose want
he is not aware.'—'Who, then, O Diotima,' I inquired,
'are philosophers, if they are neither the ignorant nor
the wise?'—'It is evident, even to a child, that they
are those intermediate persons, among whom is Love.
For Wisdom is one of the most beautiful of all things;
Love is that which thirsts for the beautiful, so that
Love is of necessity a philosopher, philosophy being
an intermediate state between ignorance and wisdom. His parentage accounts for his condition, being
the child of a wise and well provided father, and of
a mother both ignorant and poor.

" 'Such is the dæmoniacal nature, my dear Socrates;
nor do I wonder at your error concerning Love, for
you thought, as I conjecture from what you say, that
Love was not the lover but the beloved, and thence,
well concluded that he must be supremely beautiful;
for that which is the object of Love must indeed be
fair, and delicate, and perfect, and most happy; but
Love inherits, as I have declared, a totally opposite
nature.'—'Your words have persuasion in them, O
stranger,' I said; 'be it as you say. But this Love, what
advantages does he afford to men?'—'I will proceed
to explain it to you, Socrates. Love being such and so
produced as I have described, is, indeed, as you say,

the love of things which are beautiful. But if any one should ask us, saying: O Socrates and Diotima, why is Love the love of beautiful things? Or, in plainer words, what does the lover of that which is beautiful, love in the object of his love, and seek from it?'—'He seeks,' I said, interrupting her, 'the property and possession of it.'—'But that,' she replied, 'might still be met with another question. What has he, who possesses that which is beautiful?'—'Indeed, I cannot immediately reply.'—'But, if changing the beautiful for good, any one should inquire,—I ask, O Socrates, what is that which he who loves that which is good, loves in the object of his love?'—'To be in his possession,' I replied.—'And what has he who has the possession of good?'—'This question is of easier solution, he is happy.'—'Those who are happy, then, are happy through the possession; and it is useless to inquire what he desires, who desires to be happy; the question seems to have a complete reply. But do you think that this wish and this love are common to all men, and that all desire that that which is good should be forever present to them?'—'Certainly, common to all.'—'Why do we not say then, Socrates, that everyone loves? if, indeed, all love perpetually the same thing? But we say that some love, and some do not.'—'Indeed I wonder why it is so,'—'Wonder not,' said Diotima, 'for we select a particular species of love, and apply to it distinctively, the appellation of that which is universal.'

" 'Give me an example of such a select application.'—'Poetry; which is a general name signifying every cause whereby anything proceeds from that which is not, into that which is; so that the exercise of every inventive art is poetry, and all such artists poets. Yet they are not called poets, but distinguished by other names; and one portion or species of poetry, that which has relation to music and rhythm, is divided from all others, and known by the name belonging to all. For this is alone properly called poetry, and those who exercise the art of the species of poetry, poets. So with respect to Love. Love is indeed universally all that earnest desire for the possession of happiness and that which is good; the greatest and the subtlest love, and which inhabits the heart of every living being; but those who seek this object through the acquirement of wealth, or the exercise of the gymnastic arts, or philosophy, are not said to love, nor are called lovers; one species alone is called love, and those alone are said to be lovers, and to love, who seek the attainment of the universal desire through one species of love, which is peculiarly distinguished by the name belonging to the whole. It is asserted by some, that they love, who are seeking the lost half of their divided being. But I assert, that Love is neither the love of half nor of the whole, unless, my friend, it meets with that which is good; since men willingly cut off their own hands and feet, if they think that they are the cause of evil to them. Nor do they cherish and embrace that which may belong to themselves, merely because it is their own; unless, indeed, any one should choose to say, that that which is good is attached to his own nature and is his own, whilst that which is evil is foreign and accidental; but love nothing but that which is good. Does it not appear so to you?'—'Assuredly.'—'Can we then simply affirm that men love that which is good?'—'Without doubt.'—'What, then, must we not add, that, in addition to loving that which is good, they love that it should be present to themselves?'—'Indeed that must be added.'—'And not merely that it should be present, but that it should ever be present?'—'This also must be added.'

" 'Love, then, is collectively the desire in men that good should be for ever present to them.'—'Most true.'—'Since this is the general definition of Love, can you explain in what mode of attaining its object, and in what species of actions, does Love peculiarly consist?'—'If I knew what you ask, O Diotima, I should not have so much wondered at your wisdom, nor have sought you out for the purpose of deriving improvement from your instructions.'—'I will tell you,' she replied: 'Love is the desire of generation in the beautiful, both with relation to the body and the soul.'—'I must be a diviner to comprehend what you say, for, being such as I am, I confess that I do not understand it.'—'But I will explain it more clearly. The bodies and the souls of all human beings are alike pregnant with their future progeny, and when we arrive at a certain age, our nature impels us to bring forth and propagate. This nature is unable to produce in that which is deformed, but it can produce in that which is beautiful. The intercourse of the male and female in generation, a divine work, through pregnancy and production, is, as it were, something immortal in mortality. These things cannot take place in that which is incongruous; for that which is deformed is incongruous, but that which is beautiful is congruous with what is mortal and divine. Beauty is, therefore, the fate, and the goddess to generation. Wherefore, whenever that which is pregnant with the generative principle, approaches that which is beautiful, it becomes transported with delight, and is poured forth in overflowing pleasure, and propagates. But when it approaches that which is deformed it is contracted by sadness, and being repelled and checked, it does not produce, but retains unwillingly that with which it is pregnant. Wherefore, to one pregnant, and, as it were, already bursting with the

75

load of his desire, the impulse towards that which is beautiful is intense, on account of the great pain of retaining that which he has conceived. Love, then, O Socrates, is not as you imagine the love of the beautiful.'—'What, then?'—'Of generation and production in the beautiful.'—'Why then of generation?'—'Generation is something eternal and immortal in mortality. It necessarily, from what has been confessed, follows, that we must desire immortality together with what is good, since Love is the desire that good be for ever present to us. Of necessity Love must also be the desire of immortality.'

"Diotima taught me all this doctrine in the discourse we had together concerning Love; and, in addition, she inquired, 'What do you think, Socrates, is the cause of this love and desire? Do you not perceive how all animals, both those of the earth and of the air, are affected when they desire the propagation of their species, affected even to weakness and disease by the impulse of their love; first, longing to be mixed with each other, and then seeking nourishment for their offspring, so that the feeblest are ready to contend with the strongest in obedience to this law, and to die for the sake of their young, or to waste away with hunger, and do or suffer anything so that they may not want nourishment. It might be said that human beings do these things through reason, but can you explain why other animals are thus affected through love?'—I confessed that I did not know.—'Do you imagine yourself,' said she, 'to be skillful in the science of Love, if you are ignorant of these things?'—'As I said before, O Diotima, I come to you, well knowing how much I am in need of a teacher. But explain to me, I entreat you, the cause of these things, and of the other things relating to Love.'—'If,' said Diotima, 'you believe that Love is of the same nature as we have mutually agreed upon, wonder not that such are its effects. For the mortal nature seeks, so far as it is able, to become deathless and eternal. But it can only accomplish this desire by generation, which for ever leaves another new in place of the old. For, although each human being be severally said to live, and be the same from youth to old age, yet, that which is called the same, never contains within itself the same things, but always is becoming new by the loss and change of that which it possessed before; both the hair and the flesh, and the bones, and the entire body.

" 'And not only does this change take place in the body, but also with respect to the soul. Manners, morals, opinions, desires, pleasures, sorrows, fears; none of these ever remain unchanged in the same persons; but some die away, and others are produced. And, what is yet more strange is, that not only does some knowledge spring up, and another decay, and that we are never the same with respect to our knowledge, but that each several object of our thoughts suffers the same revolution. That which is called meditation, or the exercise of memory, is the science of the escape or departure of memory; for, forgetfulness is the going out of knowledge; and meditation, calling up a new memory in the place of that which has departed, preserves knowledge; so that, though forever displaced and restored, it seems to be the same. In this manner every thing mortal is preserved: not that it is constant and eternal, like that which is divine; but that in the place of what has grown old and is departed, it leaves another new like that which it was itself. By this contrivance, O Socrates, does what is mortal, the body and all other things, partake of immortality; that which is immortal, is immortal in another manner. Wonder not, then, if everything by nature cherishes that which was produced from itself, for this earnest Love is a tendency towards eternity.'

"Having heard this discourse, I was astonished, and asked, 'Can these things be true, O wisest Diotima?' And she, like an accomplished sophist, said, 'Know well, O Socrates, that if you only regard that love of glory which inspires men, you will wonder at your own unskillfulness in not having discovered all that I now declare. Observe with how vehement a desire they are affected to become illustrious and to prolong their glory into immortal time, to attain which object, far more ardently than for the sake of their children, all men are ready to engage in many dangers, and expend their fortunes, and submit to any labors and incur any death. Do you believe that Alcestis would have died in the place of Admetus, or Achilles for the revenge of Patroclus, or Codrus for the kingdom of his posterity, if they had not believed that the immortal memory of their actions, which we now cherish, would have remained after their death? Far otherwise; all such deeds are done for the sake of ever-living virtue, and this immortal glory which they have obtained; and inasmuch as any one is of an excellent nature, so much the more is he impelled to attain this reward. For they love what is immortal.

" 'Those whose bodies alone are pregnant with this principle of immortality are attracted by women, seeking through the production of children what they imagine to be happiness and immortality and an enduring remembrance; but they whose souls are far more pregnant than their bodies, conceive and produce that which is more suitable to the soul. What is suitable to the soul? Intelligence, and every other power and excellence of the mind; of which all poets, and all other artists who are creative and inventive, are the authors. The greatest and most admirable wisdom is that which regulates the government of families and states, and which is called moderation and justice. Whosoever, therefore, from his youth feels his soul pregnant with the conception of these excellencies, is divine; and when due time arrives, desires to bring forth; and wandering about, he seeks the beautiful in which he may propagate what he has conceived; for there is no generation in that which is deformed; he embraces those bodies which are beautiful rather than those which are deformed, in obedience to the principle which is within him, which is ever seeking to perpetuate itself. And if he meets, in conjunction with loveliness of form, a beautiful, generous, and gentle soul, he embraces both at once, and immediately undertakes to educate this object of his love, and is inspired with an overflowing persuasion to declare what is virtue, and what he ought to be who would attain to its possession, and what are the duties which it exacts. For, by the intercourse with, and as it were, the very touch of that which is beautiful, he brings forth and produces what he had formerly conceived; and nourishes and educates that which is thus produced together with the object of his love, whose image, whether absent or present, is never divided from his mind. So that those who are thus united are linked by a nobler community and a firmer love, as being the common parents of a lovelier and more endearing progeny than the parents of other children. And every one who considers what posterity Homer and Hesiod, and the other great poets, have left behind them, the sources of their own immortal memory and renown, or what children of his soul Lycurgus has appointed to be the guardians, not only of Lacedæmon, but of all Greece; or what an illustrious progeny of laws Solon has produced, and how many admirable achievements, both among the Greeks and Barbarians, men have left as the pledges of that love which subsisted between them and the beautiful, would choose rather to be the parent of such children than those in a human shape. For divine honors have often been rendered to them on account of such children, but on account of those in human shape, never.

" 'Your own meditation, O Socrates, might perhaps have initiated you in all these things which I have already taught you on the subject of Love. But those perfect and sublime ends to which these are only the means, I know not that you would have been competent to discover. I will declare them, therefore, and will render them as intelligible as possible: do you meanwhile strain all your attention to trace the obscure depth of the subject. He who aspires to love rightly, ought from his earliest youth to seek an intercourse with beautiful forms, and first to make a single form the object of his love, and therein to generate intellectual excellences. He ought, then, to consider that beauty in whatever form it resides is the brother of that beauty which subsists in another form; and if he ought to pursue that which is beautiful in form, it would be absurd to imagine that beauty is not one and the same thing in all forms, and would therefore remit much of his ardent preference towards one, through his perception of the multitude of claims upon his love. In addition, he would consider the beauty which is in souls more excellent than that which is in form. So that one endowed with an admirable soul, even though the flower of the form were withered, would suffice him as the object of his love and care, and the companion with whom he might seek and produce such conclusions as tend to the improvement of youth; so that it might be led to observe the beauty and the conformity which there is in the observation of its duties and the laws, and to esteem little the mere beauty of the outward form. He would then conduct his pupil to science, so that he might look upon the loveliness of wisdom; and that contemplating thus the universal beauty, no longer would he unworthily and meanly enslave himself to the attractions of one form in love, nor one subject of discipline or science, but would turn toward the wide ocean of intellectual beauty, and from the sight of the lovely and majestic forms which it contains, would abundantly bring forth his conceptions in philosophy; until, strengthened and confirmed, he should at length steadily contemplate one science, which is the science of this universal beauty.

" 'Attempt, I entreat you, to mark what I say with as keen an observation as you can. He who has been disciplined to this point in Love, by contemplating beautiful objects gradually, and in their order, now arriving at the end of all that concerns Love, on a sudden beholds a beauty wonderful in its nature. This is it, O Socrates, for the sake of which all the former labors were endured. It is eternal, unproduced, indestructible; neither subject to increase nor decay: not, like other things, partly beautiful and partly deformed; not at one time beautiful and at another time not; not beautiful in relation to one thing and deformed in relation to another; not here beautiful and there deformed; not beautiful in the estimation of one person and deformed in that of another; nor can this supreme beauty be figured to the imagination like a beautiful face, or beautiful hands, or any portion of the body, nor like any discourse, nor any science. Nor does it subsist in any other that lives or is, either in earth, or in heaven, or in any other place; but it is eternally uniform and consistent, and monoeidic with itself. All other things are beautiful through a participation of it, with this condition, that although they are subject to production and decay, it never becomes more or less, or endures any change. When anyone, ascending from a correct system of Love, begins to contemplate this supreme beauty, he already touches the consummation of his labor. For such as discipline themselves upon this system, or are conducted by another beginning to ascend through these transitory objects which are beautiful, towards that which is beauty itself, proceeding as on steps from the love of one form to that of two, and from that of two, to that of all forms which are beautiful; and from beautiful forms to beautiful habits and institutions, and from institutions to beautiful doctrines; until, from the meditation of many doctrines, they arrive at that which is nothing else than the doctrine of the supreme beauty itself, in the knowledge and contemplation of which at length they repose.

" 'Such a life as this, my dear Socrates,' exclaimed the stranger Prophetess, 'spent in the contemplation of the beautiful, is the life for men to live; which if you chance ever to experience, you will esteem far beyond gold and rich garments, and even those persons whom you and many others now gaze on with astonishment, and are prepared neither to eat nor drink so that you may behold and live for ever with these objects of your love! What then shall we imagine to be the aspect of the supreme beauty itself, simple, pure, uncontaminated with the intermixture of human flesh and colors, and all other idle and unreal shapes attendant on mortality; the divine, the original, the supreme, the monoeidic beautiful itself? What must be the life of him who dwells with and gazes on that which it becomes us all to seek? Think you not that to him alone is accorded the prerogative of bringing forth, not images and shadows of virtue, for he is in contact not with a shadow but with reality; with virtue itself, in the production and nourishment of which he becomes dear to the Gods, and if such a privilege is conceded to any human being, himself immortal.'

"Such, O Phædrus, and my other friends, was what Diotima said. And being persuaded by her words, I have since occupied myself in attempting to persuade others, that it is not easy to find a better assistant than Love in seeking to communicate immortality to our human natures. Wherefore I exhort everyone to honor Love; I hold him in honor, and chiefly exercise myself in amatory matters, and exhort others to do so; and now and ever do I praise the power and excellence of Love, in the best manner that I can. Let this discourse, if it pleases you, Phædrus, be considered as an encomium of Love; or call it by what other name you will."

And what of the man himself who thus challenges our thinking? No more beautiful and penetrating picture can be imagined than what follows next in *The Symposium*. Socrates' encomium of Love finished, the dinner is interrupted by a band of uninvited and drunken revelers, Alcibiades among them, who typically of the informal life of the day settle down for the rest of the evening. Being urged to speak in praise of Socrates, Alcibiades begins as follows:

"I will begin the praise of Socrates by comparing him to a certain statue. Perhaps he will think that this statue is introduced for the sake of ridicule, but I assure you that it is necessary for the illustration of truth. I assert, then, that Socrates is exactly like those Silenuses that sit in the sculptors' shops, and which are carved holding flutes or pipes, but which, when divided in two, are found to contain within the images of the gods. I assert that Socrates is like the satyr Marsyas. That your form and appearance are like these satyrs, I think that even you will not venture to deny; and how like you are to them in all other things, now hear. Are you not scornful and petulant? If you deny this, I will bring witnesses. Are you not a piper, and far more wonderful a one than he? For Marsyas, and whoever now pipes the music that he taught (for the melodies of Olympus are derived from Marsyas who taught them), enchants men through the power of the mouth. For if any musician, be he skillful or not, awakens this music, it alone enables him to retain the minds of men, and from the divinity of its nature makes evident those who are in want of the gods and initiation. You differ only from Marsyas in this circumstance, that you effect without instruments, by mere words, all that he can do. For when we hear Pericles, or any other accomplished orator, deliver a discourse, no one, as it were, cares anything about it. But when anyone hears you, or even your words related by another, though ever so rude and unskillful a speaker, be that person a woman, man or child, we are struck and retained, as it were, by the discourse clinging to our mind.

"If I was not afraid that I am a great deal too drunk, I would confirm to you by an oath the strange effects which I assure you I have suffered from his words, and suffer still; for when I hear him speak, my heart leaps up far more than the hearts of those who celebrate the Corybantic mysteries; my tears are poured out as he talks, a thing I have seen happen to many others beside myself. I have heard Pericles and other excellent orators, and have been pleased with their discourses, but I suffered nothing of this kind; nor was my soul ever on those occasions disturbed and filled with self-reproach, as if it were slavishly laid prostrate. But this Marsyas here has often affected me in the way I describe, until the life which I lead seemed hardly worth living. Do not deny it, Socrates, for I well know that if even now I chose to listen to you, I could not resist, but should again suffer the same effects. For, my friends, he forces me to confess that while I myself am still in want of many things, I neglect my own necessities, and attend to those of the Athenians. I stop my ears, therefore, as from the Sirens, and flee away as fast as possible, that I may not sit down beside him and grow old in listening to his talk. For this man has reduced me to feel the sentiment of shame, which I imagine no one would readily believe was in me; he alone inspires me with remorse and awe. For I feel in his presence my incapacity of refuting what he says, or of refusing to do that which he directs; but when I depart from him, the glory which the multitude confers overwhelms me. I escape, therefore, and hide myself from him, and when I see him I am overwhelmed with humiliation, because I have neglected to do what I have confessed to him ought to be done; and often and often have I wished that he were no longer to be seen among men. But if that were to happen, I well know that I should suffer far greater pain; so that where I can turn, or what I can do with this man, I know not. All this have I and many others suffered from the pipings of this satyr.

"And observe, how like he is to what I said, and what a wonderful power he possesses. Know that there is not one of you who is aware of the real nature of Socrates; but since I have begun, I will make him plain to you. You observe how passionately Socrates affects the intimacy of those who are beautiful, and how ignorant he professes himself to be; appearances in themselves excessively Silenic. This, my friends, is the external form with which, like one of the sculptured Silenuses, he has clothed himself; for if you open him, you will find within admirable temperance and wisdom. For he cares not for mere beauty, but despises more than any one can imagine all external possessions, whether it be beauty or wealth, or glory, or any other thing for which the multitude felicitates the possessor. He esteems these things and us who honor them, as nothing, and lives among men, making all the objects of their admiration the playthings of his irony. But I know not if any one of you have ever seen the divine images which are within, when he has been opened and is serious. I have seen them, and they are so supremely beautiful, so golden, so divine, and wonderful, that everything which Socrates commands surely ought to be obeyed, even like the voice of a God.

"At one time we were fellow soldiers, and had our mess together in the camp before Potidæa. Socrates there overcame not only me, but everyone beside, in endurance of toils: when, as often happens in a campaign, we were reduced to few provisions, there were none who could sustain hunger like Socrates; and when we had plenty, he alone seemed to enjoy our military fare. He never drank much willingly, but when he was compelled he conquered all even in that to which he was least accustomed; and what is most astonishing, no person ever saw Socrates drunk either then or at any other time. In the depth of winter (and the winters there are excessively rigid) he sustained calmly incredible hardships; and amongst other things, whilst the frost was intolerably severe, and no one went out of their tents, or if they went out, wrapt themselves up carefully, and put fleeces under their feet, and bound their legs with hairy skins, Socrates went out only with the same cloak on that he usually wore, and walked barefoot upon the ice; more easily, indeed, than those who had sandalled themselves so delicately: so that the soldiers thought that he did it to mock their want of fortitude. It would indeed be worth while to commemorate all that this brave man did and endured in that expedition. In one instance he was seen early in the morning, standing in one place wrapt in meditation; and as he seemed not to be able to unravel the subject of his thoughts, he still continued to stand as inquiring and discussing within himself, and when noon came, the soldiers observed him, and said to one another—'Socrates has been standing there thinking, ever since the morning.' At last some Ionians came to the spot, and having supped, as it was summer, bringing their blankets, they lay down to sleep in the cool; they observed that Socrates continued to stand there the whole night until morning, and that, when the sun rose, he saluted it with a prayer and departed.

"I ought not to omit what Socrates is in battle. For in that battle after which the generals decreed to me the prize of courage, Socrates alone of all men was the savior of my life, standing by me when I had fallen and was wounded, and preserving both myself and my arms from the hands of the enemy. On that occasion I entreated the generals to decree the prize, as it was most due, to him. And this, O Socrates, you cannot deny, that the generals wishing to conciliate a person of my rank, desired to give me the prize, you were far more earnestly desirous than the generals that this glory should be attributed not to yourself but me.

"But to see Socrates when our army was defeated

and scattered in flight at Delium, was a spectacle worthy to behold. On that occasion I was among the cavalry, and he on foot, heavily armed. After the total rout of our troops, he and Laches retreated together; I came up by chance, and seeing them, bade them be of good cheer, for that I would not leave them. As I was on horseback, and therefore less occupied by a regard of my own situation, I could better observe than at Potidæa the beautiful spectacle exhibited by Socrates on this emergency. How superior was he to Laches in presence of mind and courage! Your representation of him on the stage, O Aristophanes, was not wholly unlike his real self on this occasion, for he walked and darted his regards around with a majestic composure, looking tranquilly both on his friends and enemies; so that it was evident to every one, even from afar, that whoever should venture to attack him would encounter a desperate resistance. He and his companion thus departed in safety; for those who are scattered in flight are pursued and killed, whilst men hesitate to touch those who exhibit such a countenance as that of Socrates even in defeat.

"Many other and most wonderful qualities might well be praised in Socrates; but such as these might singly be attributed to others. But that which is unparalleled in Socrates, is, that he is unlike, and above comparison, with all other men, whether those who have lived in ancient times, or those who exist now. For it may be conjectured, that Brasidas and many others are such as was Achilles. Pericles deserves comparison with Nestor and Antenor; and other excellent persons of various times may, with probability, be drawn into comparison with each other. But to such a singular man as this, both himself and his discourses are so uncommon, no one, should he seek, would find a parallel among the present or the past generations of mankind; unless they should say that he resembled those with whom I lately compared him, for, assuredly, he and his discourses are like nothing but the Silenus and the Satyrs. At first I forgot to make you observe how like his discourses are to those Satyrs when they are opened, for, if any one will listen to the talk of Socrates, it will appear to him at first extremely ridiculous; the phrases and expressions which he employs, fold around his exterior the skin, as it were, of a rude and wanton Satyr. He is always talking about great market-asses, and brass-founders, and leather-cutters, and skin-dressers; and this is his perpetual custom, so that any dull and unobservant person might easily laugh at his discourse. But if any one should see it opened, as it were, and get within the sense of his words, he would then find that they alone of all that enters into the mind of man to utter, had a profound and persuasive meaning, and that they were most divine; and that they presented to the mind innumerable images of every excellence, and that they tended towards objects of the highest moment, or rather towards all that he who seeks the possession of what is supremely beautiful and good need regard as essential to the accomplishment of his ambition.

"These are the things, my friends, for which I praise Socrates."

V

LIFE

HIGH SUCCESS in many fields of endeavor, together with continuing experimentation, must be the principal explanation of the dynamic spirit of the Athenians in the fifth century B.C. The experience gained by the stone-cutters and other ordinary laborers on the new buildings was, in its way, as educational as the festivals of state and demes. Since over sixty days in the year were devoted to these exhibitions, with the choruses requiring the services of two thousand boys and men, most Athenians were more than mere spectators in the theater. They participated actively in a living literature at a time when artists and writers from the entire Greek world tended to congregate in Athens. The central fact about Periclean Athens, however, was the full participation of its citizens in the government of city and empire.

The Athenians might fairly claim to be good critics of art and literature and governmental policy, but since they were also innovators on a grand scale, only the future could tell whether others would be frightened into hostile action. Though the Peloponnesian League southward, like Thebes to the north, was oligarchical, these states did in fact represent the old, conventional form of life in Greece and consequently they were able to proclaim Athens a tyrant. Within the empire itself, this feeling was limited to the local aristocracies at first, because Athens supported the democratic factions in the member states.

The imperial tribute helped the masses share in government, festival and public works, but since the Athenians were able to continue, and even to increase, the payments for public services in the next century, when the empire had disappeared, the tribute clearly was not essential; it did, however, make mass participation easier, and it set a fashion. The institution of slavery also created a certain necessary leisure, but slavery in Greece was on a far more limited scale than in Roman and later days. The conclusion is inescapable that Athenian success was due primarily to the vision and work of the people themselves. Through the generations they had labored consistently to win a fuller and a more urban democracy, and the realization of it coincided with victorious war and empire.

The chief fruits, however, went to the men of Athens. It was a masculine age, far more so than in the preceding century or in the one to follow. Respectable women remained at home and appeared in public chiefly at the time of funerals, weddings, and festivals. Their place in the society of men was taken by better educated women, called *hetæræ* or companions, who came from outside Athens, such as Pericles' famous *hetæra,* Aspasia of Miletus in Asia Minor. Because of his own law which required that both parents be native born, their son was excluded from the franchise until the Assembly gave it to him by a special vote.

It was proper, so the Athenians thought, for the citizen alone to have political and property rights, since on him fell the chief duty of defending the state. And because the ownership of land was an automatic sign, so to speak, that the individual was a citizen, farming enjoyed a primacy among the various occupations. The naturally conservative instincts of the small, middle-class farmer were much the same as those of the landed nobility and gave to the state a stability which was unusual in contemporary Greece.

Agriculture was the economic basis of Athens, as it was of all ancient societies. From the Attic farms came the wine, oil, wheat, and barley, the wool, pork, cheese, and greens necessary to sustain life, though much wheat had to be imported, chiefly from the regions around the Black Sea. Dried fish and timber for shipbuilding were other significant imports. A tax was placed on these as on the exports, such as the shields and jewelry produced by small shops and the pottery made from the famous Attic clay. The marble from Mt. Pentelicus was an important natural resource, as were the silver mines of Laurium at the tip of the Attic peninsula and the gold and silver mines of Mt. Pangæus in northern Greece, which Athens controlled. There was no direct tax until the Peloponnesian War, when a property tax was introduced, but the rich were subject to special levies, such as the necessity of training a chorus. The economy was relatively simple, and the advantage of maintaining the empire and its tribute can be readily imagined.

Agriculture, industry, and government took up the time of most citizens, so that business and trade fell largely into the hands of aliens who were permanently domiciled in the city. These were known as metics, and though they had neither political nor property rights and were required to perform military service and pay a special tax, they were happy to have the opportunity. Since each state proudly maintained its own system of coinage and weights, trade ran into various barriers, though of course the worst deterrents were war and piracy. For a time the Athenian navy practically swept piracy from the sea, and this was most fortunate, because the mountains and poor roads of Greece made trade and travel by land very difficult.

The slaves, too, enjoyed a happier life than has ordinarily been their lot, provided we except those state slaves who were worked like animals in mine and quarry. The ordinary Athenian might have half a dozen slaves, and together on the farm or in the shop they labored. On his own time the slave could work for hire and eventually purchase his freedom. He then assumed the status of a metic. We still possess an inscription, dealing with the construction of the Erechtheum, which vividly illustrates the equality of the various classes. Twenty citizens, thirty-five metics and sixteen slaves are mentioned, and each of them, as well as the architect, received a drachma a day, about twice the daily cost of living for an unmarried person. (To say that a drachma is approximately equivalent to twenty American cents conveys no real idea of comparative values and costs.)

The population of ancient states is notoriously difficult to estimate, and particularly so for the Greeks who, unlike the Romans, did not take a census. But a fair guess for Periclean Athens would be 150,000 citizens, 35,000 metics, and 80,000 slaves, counting men, women, and children in each case. Probably it was a predominantly youthful population, though the person who survived disease and warfare till he was sixty had a fair chance of exceeding the Biblical three score and ten.

If we exclude the few rich families, the extremes of wealth and poverty to which we are accustomed were conspicuously absent in ancient Athens. Not only was life simple, it was relatively uncomplicated. Tradition dictated a house small in size, for originally, of course, all

Greek towns had been small, with the houses clustered together for safety's sake within a short circuit wall. Even
when the town grew and the city height or Acropolis no
longer sufficed as a refuge and became a showplace with
temples to the gods, and larger circuit walls were thrown
up, tradition still dictated the small house. The suspicion
with which each Greek viewed his neighbor prevented all
but the most daring to exhibit any special wealth. Besides, the warm climate invited outdoor life, and the democratic, masculine spirit of the time caused men to look
on their abodes more as houses than as homes.

The mudbrick houses of the Athenians rose beside their
narrow, crooked streets and presented a bleak exterior to
the passerby. Life centered around the open-air court-
yard within and if there was a second story, the bedrooms
were placed there. The chairs, tables, and other furniture
of the house were in keeping with the general simplicity,
for the Greeks customarily developed few types of practi-
cal things, but these they made, in the first instance, useful and then beautiful. No further experimentation
seemed desirable. The same sort of oblong clothing, a
short woolen garment known as a *chiton,* was worn by
men for generations.

Shopping at Athens was done by the men, unless the
day's work or governmental duties were too pressing. An
early morning glass of wine sufficed for breakfast, and
then the Athenian set off for one or more of the markets.
Fish, oil, metalwork, clothing and so on were sold either
in their own markets or in specific sections of one, a custom that has long characterized the Near East. Water-
clocks and sundials gave the Athenian the time of day as
he strolled about town, and barbershops provided the
gossip. (The story goes that a Macedonian king, when

asked how he would have his hair cut, replied, "In silence.") Lunch was generally a family affair, after which the Athenian might go to the gymnasium to engage in sports or conversation, for, unlike the Roman, he took neither a large meal nor a long siesta. Evenings were spent quietly at home, unless guests had been invited to dinner. The guests were almost certainly men. They reclined on couches and reached for the food that had been placed in front of them on tables. Thus the different courses came to be known as first and second table; it was customary to drop "leftovers" on the floor, where dogs, who had been eagerly lying under the couches, would get them. When the meal was finished, the king of the symposium, as he was called, would be elected, and it was his task, first, to decide how much water should be mixed with the wine, and then to choose the topic of conversation for the evening.

A simpler civilized life would be difficult to imagine, but, then, the Greeks are famous for their extraordinary combination of high thinking with plain living. Much of an Athenian's time was normally spent in the business of government, which surely was the most important factor in his education. For a meeting of the Assembly he took himself to the Pnyx, a hill to the west of the Acropolis and the Areopagus (whence St. Paul addressed the Athenians centuries later, in the days of Rome's dominion). Other state business was conducted in the Agora, just to the north of the Acropolis.

The Agora was the civic center of the city. An important street, that of the Panathenæa, ran through it, from the Dipylon (Double) Gate in the city wall to the Acropolis. The state procession that went along this street in August was immortalized by the Parthenon frieze. Various temples—such as those of Ares, the god of war, and Hephæstus,

95

the god of metalworkers—and sanctuaries dominated the Agora, for it was a sacred area, and a person purified himself at basins of holy water on entering. Altars to the gods stood here and there, and from one of them, that of the Twelve Gods, was measured the distance to the towns of Attica. The Athenian Agora was striking also for its many statues. Eventually concerts were presented in a regular music hall, the Odeon, and a library was built from which this inscription has survived: "No book may be taken out. The Library will be open from morning to midday."

A good deal of conventional business was conducted in the Agora, especially in the shady stoas or colonnades. Of first importance, however, were the governmental buildings: the civic offices, mint, law courts, the headquarters of the Ten Generals, the Council House, and the Tholos. The Tholos, a circular building, was the actual center of the Athenian government, for certain officials ate and slept there, ever ready for an emergency. The whole area of the Agora has only recently been uncovered by the excavations of the American School of Classical Studies at Athens, a triumphant piece of scholarship involving the purchase of twenty-six acres in the midst of the busy, modern city, and the removal of 300,000 tons of earth.

The Greeks stood at the beginning of European history, with no comparable achievement in their past. It would have been easy for Sophocles to celebrate the rapid and extraordinary rise of his fellow Athenians, but in his *Antigone* this supreme example of a tragic poet who, in the words of Matthew Arnold, "saw life steadily and saw it whole" preferred, rather typically of his race, to sing of Man instead:

Life

Strophe 1

CHORUS: *Many are the wonders of the world,*
And none so wonderful as Man.
Over the waters wan
His storm-vext bark he steers,
While the fierce billows break
Round his path, and o'er his head:
And the Earth-mother, first of gods,
The ageless, the indomitable,
With his ploughing to and fro
He wearieth, year by year:
In the deep furrow toil the patient mules.

Antistrophe 1

The birds o' the air he snares and takes,
All the light-hearted fluttering race:
And tribes of savage beasts,
And creatures of the deep,
Meshed in his woven toils,
Own the master-mind of man.
Free lives of upland and of wild
By human arts are curbed and tamed:
See the horse's shaggy neck
Submissive to the yoke—
And strength untired of mountain-roaming bulls.

Strophe 2

Language withal he learnt,
And Thought that as the wind is free,
And aptitudes of civic life:
Ill-lodged no more he lies,
His roof the sky, the earth his bed,
Screened now from piercing frost and pelting rain;
All-fertile in resource, resourceless never
Meets he the morrow; only death
He wants the skill to shun:

97

But many a fell disease the healer's art hath foiled.

Antistrophe 2
So soaring far past hope,
The wise inventiveness of man
Finds diverse issues, good and ill:
If from their course he wrests
The firm foundations of the state,
Laws, and the justice he is sworn to keep,
High in the city, citiless I deem him,
Dealing with baseness: overbold,
May he my hearth avoid,
Nor let my thoughts with his, who does such
  deeds, agree!

And what poet has ever caught better than Æschylus the emergence of man from savagery, his problems and his vast achievement? Here is Prometheus speaking in *Prometheus Bound:*

Yet to these upstart gods who else but I
Laid down the roles—ah, that ye *know; no more*
I'll tell the selfsame tale, but harken ye
To this: the story of man's *suffering,*
How without language, witless hitherto,
I gave him mind, the use of intellect,
All, all I'll tell you, witnessing the love
I bore humanity.

First know ye then
That men had eyes and saw not, ears they had
But could not hear. Like figures in a dream
They lived their long lives out; by merest chance
All things were done. Never did sun-dried brick
Or axe-hewn beam rear them a sheltering home.

Life

Nay, in dark caves they dwelt like creeping ants,
Crawling through sunless ways. No witness sure
Had they of winter's coming or the times
Of flowering summer or of autumn's blaze.
Ignorant they of all things till I came
And told them of the rising of the stars
And their dark settings, taught them numbers too,
The queen of knowledge. I instructed them
How to join letters, making them their slaves
To serve the memory, mother of the muse.
'Twas I that first compelled beneath the yoke
The beasts of burden, thence to be for man
Sharer of all his toil, harnessed the horse
Unto the chariot to obey the rein
And be henceforth the pride of opulence.
I too, I and no other, bade them guide
Sail-driven ships across the boundless sea.

. . . . .
Greatest I deem is this: if hitherto
Sickness befell, no cure was known on earth,
No strengthening food, no ointment soothing pain,
No healing draught: man without kindly drugs
Wasted and died. Then I came and revealed
The mystery of potions that could cure
Every disease. Nor was this all. I taught
Blind mortals many a sure, unerring way
To read the future, what each dream foretold,
How to interpret voices of the air
And portents by the way, the flight of birds,
Wherein lay happiness, where evil lurked,
What elements combined in harmony,
And which were hostile, warring evermore
On one another, how to read aright
The smoking entrails, what the gods decreed
The auspicious color of the gall, what shape
Within the lobe, curious, intricate,

Augured most happily. I guided man
In all the science of the sacrifice,
To wrap the members in the victim's fat
And read the darkling symbols of the flame.
So I instructed him, and furthermore,
Who else but I, delving beneath the earth,
Brought first to light the treasures hidden deep,
The wealth of copper, iron, silver, gold?
None else, I know full well, who would not be
A babbling fool, can claim priority.

The tragedy of it all was that the freshness of man's
life at Athens—the democratic zest and enthusiasm, the
flair for experimentation, the devotion to reason, at least
on the part of some—could not continue to develop at a
normal pace. But a long and terrible war brought to an
end the natural flowering of a civilization which, as Toynbee has expressed it, "still outshines every other civilization that has ever come into existence up to the present."
Surveying the stirring events of his own generation,
Thucydides made this estimate of the friend who stood
out above all others:

Worst of all, instead of enjoying peace, the Athenians
were now at war. The popular indignation was not
pacified until they had fined Pericles; but, soon afterward, with the usual fickleness of a multitude, they
elected him general and committed all their affairs
to his charge. Their private sorrows were beginning to
be less acutely felt, and for a time of public need they
thought that there was no man like him. During the
peace while he was at the head of affairs he ruled
with prudence; under his guidance Athens was safe,
and reached the height of her greatness in his time.
When the war began he showed that here too he had

formed a true estimate of the Athenian power. He survived the commencement of hostilities two years and six months; and, after his death, his foresight was even better appreciated than during his life. For he had told the Athenians that if they would be patient and would attend to their navy, and not seek to enlarge their dominion while the war was going on, nor imperil the existence of the city, they would be victorious; but they did all that he told them not to do, and in matters which seemingly had nothing to do with the war, from motives of private ambition and private interest they adopted a policy which had disastrous effects in respect both of themselves and of their allies; their measures, had they been successful, would only have brought honor and profit to individuals, and, when unsuccessful, crippled the city in the conduct of the war. The reason of the difference was that he, deriving authority from his capacity and acknowledged worth, being also a man of transparent integrity, was able to control the multitude in a free spirit; he led them rather than was led by them; for, not seeking power by dishonest arts, he had no need to say pleasant things, but, on the strength of his own high character, could venture to oppose and even to anger them. When he saw them unseasonably elated and arrogant, his words humbled and awed them; and, when they were depressed by groundless fears, he sought to reanimate their confidence. Thus Athens, though still in name a democracy, was in fact ruled by her greatest citizen. But his successors were more on an equality with one another, and, each one struggling to be first himself, they were ready to sacrifice the whole conduct of affairs to the whims of the people. Such weakness in a great and imperial city led to many errors.

VI

WAR

IF WE ARE TO determine the cause of the Peloponnesian War (431–404 B.C.), which converted Greece overnight into a disillusioned society striving somehow to maintain the pattern of the past, we must avoid a familiar and pleasant approach. This is to assume that the major share of the blame must fall, not on democratic Athens and its maritime empire, but on the militaristic, oligarchical land empire of Sparta. It is quite true that Athens and Sparta were very different. The Spartans, or Lacedæmonians as they were also called, were living on their past in the valley of Laconia, deliberately cut off from trade and the normal ways of civilization. They belonged to the Dorian branch of the Greek race, were narrow in outlook, monarchical and regimented in their government and life. They headed the powerful Peloponnesian League, though the more progressive Corinthians often found it necessary to remind the Spartans of their obligation to lead. The Athenians, on the other hand, were Ionian Greeks, democratic and radical, the cultural leaders of Greece, the head, of course, of a sea empire.

Here was a dualism into which Greece had settled and might have continued, had not the restless, innovating Athenians aroused so much fear. The Corinthians expressed the general sentiment of Greece at a congress held at Sparta just before the outbreak of the war. In the report of Thucydides, they saw the chief protagonists in this light:

"And you have never considered what manner of men are these Athenians with whom you will have to fight, and how utterly unlike yourselves. They are revolutionary, equally quick in the conception and in the execution of every new plan; while you are conservative—careful only to keep what you have, originating nothing, and not acting even when action is most urgent. They are bold beyond their strength; they run risks which prudence would condemn; and in the midst of misfortune they are full of hope. Whereas it is your nature, though strong, to act feebly; when your plans are most prudent, to distrust them; and when calamities come upon you, to think that you will never be delivered from them. They are impetuous, and you are dilatory; they are always abroad, and you are always at home. For they hope to gain something by leaving their homes; but you are afraid that any new enterprise may imperil what you have already. When conquerors, they pursue their victory to the utmost; when defeated, they fall back the least. Their bodies they devote to their country as though they belonged to other men; their true self is their mind, which is most truly their own when employed in her service. When they do not carry out an intention which they have formed, they seem to themselves to have sustained a personal bereavement; when an enterprise succeeds, they have gained a mere installment of what is to come; but if they fail, they at once conceive new hopes and so fill up the void. With them alone to hope is to have, for they lose not a moment in the execution of an idea. This is the lifelong task, full of danger and toil, which they are always imposing upon themselves. None enjoy their good things less, because they are always seeking for more. To do their duty is their only holiday, and they deem the quiet of inaction to be as disagreeable as the most tiresome business. If a man should say of them, in a word, that they were born neither to have peace themselves nor to allow peace to other men, he would simply speak the truth."

The Athenian envoys, who were present, began their candid reply by referring to their victory over the Persians:

"Considering, Lacedæmonians, the energy and sagacity which we then displayed, do we deserve to be so bitterly hated by the other Hellenes merely because we have an empire? That empire was not acquired by force; but you would not stay and make an end of the Barbarian, and the allies came of their own accord and asked us to be their leaders. The subsequent development of our power was originally forced upon us by circumstances; fear was our first motive; afterwards honor, and then interest stepped in. And when we had incurred the hatred of most of our allies; when some of them had already revolted and been subjugated, and you were no longer the friends to us which you once had been, but suspicious and ill-disposed, how could we without great risk relax our hold? For the cities as fast as they fell away from us would have gone over to you. And no man is to be reproached who seizes every possible advantage when the danger is so great.

"At all events, Lacedæmonians, we may retort that you, in the exercise of your supremacy, manage the cities of Peloponnesus to suit your own views; and that if you, and not we, had persevered in the command of the allies long enough to be hated, you would have been quite as intolerable to them as we are, and would have been compelled, for the sake of your own safety, to rule with a strong hand. An empire was offered to us: can you wonder that, acting as human nature always will, we accepted it and refused to give it up again, constrained by three all-powerful motives, honor, fear, interest? We are not the first who have aspired to rule; the world has ever held that the weaker must be kept down by the stronger. And we think that we are worthy of power; and there was a time when you thought so too; but now, when you mean expediency you talk about justice. Did justice ever deter any one from taking by force whatever he could? Men who indulge the natural ambition of empire deserve credit if they are in any degree more careful of justice than they need be. How moderate we are would speedily appear if others took our place; indeed our very moderation, which should be our glory, has been unjustly converted into a reproach."

Long before the outbreak of war Pericles had taken various steps to make Athens invincible. He recognized, for example, that the man power of Athens did not suffice for a regular army, and that such soldiers as there were, must be employed chiefly to guard the approaches to Attica and the city itself. All available men were needed for the fleet, on which would devolve the double duty of maintaining the empire and importing the necessary supplies of food. Since, however, Athens was not directly on the sea, a hostile enemy might camp before its walls and starve it into submission. This explains Pericles' extraordinary action in building Long Walls from Athens to its harbor, Piræus, four and a half miles distant. Now, in case of war, the population of Attica might be removed into the city, and so long as the fleet controlled the sea, Athens could outlast a siege.

Athens imported many of her supplies from Greek Sicily, which was Dorian in blood and sympathy and

would surely be hostile in time of war. In order to elim-
inate Athenian dependence on Sicily, Pericles founded a
colony at Thurii, a remarkably fertile spot in southern
Italy, but the new foundation was so immense that people feared Athens might have more general designs on
the West. Not much later Pericles planted a large colony
—Amphipolis or "Double City"—in northern Greece at
the crossing of the River Strymon. It controlled the route
to the gold and silver mines of Mt. Pangæus and to Byzantium on the Bosporus, and could keep an eye on the
Athenian interests in that area. During the same year,
moreover, Pericles made a grand naval parade around the
Black Sea, to impress that important granary with the
power of Athens.

Nearer home Pericles built up a financial reserve at
Athens, something which the Peloponnesians lacked altogether. In vain the conservatives opposed him. The best
they could do was to bring about the exile of three friends,
Damonides, Pericles' instructor in music, Anaxagoras the
philosopher, and the great sculptor Pheidias, who was
convicted of embezzling gold and ivory intended for the
statue of Athena Parthenos. Pericles himself was unassail-
able, however.

The activities of Athens east and west suggested that
there was no limit to her ambition. Her control of ports
on the Corinthian Gulf particularly alarmed Corinth,
while her severe treatment of recalcitrant allies made her
appear to men everywhere as a tyrant. By comparison the
Spartans were mild and represented a traditional way
of life.

In a word, the Athenians were the new and upsetting
influence in Greece, a threat to the status quo. Thucydides
himself summed up the cause of the Peloponnesian War

as follows: "The real though unavowed cause I believe to have been the growth of the Athenian power, which terrified the Lacedæmonians and forced them into war; but the reasons publicly alleged on either side were as follows. . . . In arriving at this decision and resolving to go to war, the Lacedæmonians were influenced, not so much by the speeches of their allies, as by the fear of the Athenians and of their increasing power. For they saw the greater part of Hellas already subject to them."

Our interest in the ensuing war would be academic, excepting only its outcome, were it not for the great man who chose to write its history. Thucydides loved his native Athens, but he had the intellectual courage to be impartial and the power to dig beneath the surface and weigh the facts and forces at work. He reminds us of Sophocles and the Greek ideal, for he was also a man of action, a general during the first years of the war. Apparently he was slow in bringing reinforcements to a beleaguered city and was exiled, but this gave him the opportunity to travel around during the next twenty years and to discuss issues with participants on both sides. His *History of the Peloponnesian War* has eternal significance because, typically of great Greek thinking, he was able to raise particular events to a universal level. As he himself expressed it, "If he who desires to have before his eyes a true picture of the events which have happened, and of the like events which may be expected to happen hereafter in the order of human things, shall pronounce what I have written to be useful, then I shall be satisfied. My history is an everlasting possession, not a prize composition which is heard and forgotten."

When various overt acts, or "grievances" as they were called, made war inevitable, the Athenians found that they had available, in addition to their sailors and marines, approximately 13,000 heavy-armed foot soldiers (hoplites) and 1,000 cavalry, who were necessary for garrison duty and the siege of rebellious cities. The Peloponnesians had 24,000 hoplites and light-armed troops, while their allies of the Bœotian confederacy, headed by Thebes, commanded 10,000 hoplites and 1,000 cavalry. Pericles' strategy was to withdraw the population of Attica into Athens before the invading armies and to raid the coasts of the enemy.

Although the people grumbled about their cramped quarters and ruined farms, the plan worked well, and at the year's end Pericles delivered his famous Funeral Oration. And then a terrible plague broke out at Athens. In describing its course, Thucydides did not lose the opportunity to penetrate more deeply into man's nature:

As soon as summer returned, the Peloponnesian army, comprising as before two-thirds of the force of each confederate state, under the command of the Lacedæmonian king Archidamus, the son of Zeuxidamus, invaded Attica, where they established themselves and ravaged the country. They had not been there many days when the plague broke out at Athens for the first time. A similar disorder is said to have previously smitten many places, particularly Lemnos, but there is no record of such a pestilence occurring elsewhere, or of so great a destruction of human life. For a while physicians, in ignorance of the nature of the disease, sought to apply remedies; but it was in vain, and they themselves were among the first victims, because they oftenest came into contact with it. No human art was of any avail, and as to supplications in temples, inquiries of oracles, and the like,

they were utterly useless, and at last men were over-
powered by the calamity and gave them all up.

The disease is said to have begun south of Egypt
in Ethiopia; thence it descended into Egypt and
Libya, and after spreading over the greater part of
the Persian Empire, suddenly fell upon Athens. It first
attacked the inhabitants of Piræus, and it was supposed that the Peloponnesians had poisoned the cisterns, no conduits having as yet been made there. It
afterward reached the upper city, and then the mortality became far greater. As to its probable origin
or the causes which might or could have produced
such a disturbance of nature, every man, whether a
physician or not, will give his own opinion. But I
shall describe its actual course, and the symptoms by
which any one who knows them beforehand may
recognize the disorder should it ever reappear. For
I was myself attacked, and witnessed the sufferings of
others.

The season was admitted to have been remarkably
free from ordinary sickness; and if anybody was already ill of any other disease, it was absorbed in this.
Many who were in perfect health, all in a moment,
and without any apparent reason, were seized with
violents heats in the head and with redness and in-
flammation of the eyes. Internally the throat and the
tongue were quickly suffused with blood, and the
breath became unnatural and fetid. There followed
sneezing and hoarseness; in a short time the disorder,
accompanied by a violent cough, reached the chest;
then fastening lower down, it would move the stomach and bring on all the vomits of bile to which physicians have ever given names; and they were very
distressing. An ineffectual retching producing violent
convulsions attacked most of the sufferers; some as
soon as the previous symptoms had abated, others not

until long afterward. The body externally was not so very hot to the touch, nor yet pale; it was of a livid color inclining to red, and breaking out in pustules and ulcers. But the internal fever was intense; the sufferers could not bear to have on them even the finest linen garment; they insisted on being naked, and there was nothing which they longed for more eagerly than to throw themselves into cold water. And many of those who had no one to look after them actually plunged into the cisterns, for they were tormented by unceasing thirst, which was not in the least assuaged whether they drank little or much. They could not sleep; a restlessness which was intolerable never left them. While the disease was at its height the body, instead of wasting away, held out amid these sufferings in a marvelous manner, and either they died on the seventh or ninth day, not of weakness, for their strength was not exhausted, but of internal fever, which was the end of most; or, if they survived, then the disease descended into the bowels and there produced violent ulceration; severe diarrhoea at the same time set in, and at a later stage caused exhaustion which finally with few exceptions carried them off. For the disorder which had originally settled in the head passed gradually through the whole body, and, if a person got over the worst, would often seize the extremities and leave its mark, attacking the privy parts and the fingers and the toes; and some escaped with the loss of these, some with the loss of their eyes. Some again had no sooner recovered than they were seized with a forgetfulness of all things and knew neither themselves nor their friends.

The general character of the malady no words can describe, and the fury with which it fastened upon each sufferer was too much for human nature to endure. There was one circumstance in particular which distinguished it from ordinary diseases. The birds and animals which feed on human flesh, although so many bodies were lying unburied, either never came near them, or died if they touched them. This was proved by a remarkable disappearance of the birds of prey, which were not to be seen either about the bodies or anywhere else; while in the case of the dogs the result was even more obvious, because they live with man.

Such was the general nature of the disease: I omit many strange peculiarities which characterized individual cases. None of the ordinary sicknesses attacked anyone while it lasted, or, if they did, they ended in the plague. Some of the sufferers died from want of care, others equally who were receiving the greatest attention. No single remedy could be deemed a specific; for that which did good to one did harm to another. No constitution was of itself strong enough to resist or weak enough to escape the attacks; the disease carried off all alike and defied every mode of treatment. Most appalling was the despondency which seized upon any one who felt himself sickening; for he instantly abandoned his mind to despair and, instead of holding out, absolutely threw away his chance of life. Appalling too was the rapidity with which men caught the infection; dying like sheep if they attended on one another; and this was the principal cause of mortality. When they were afraid to visit one another, the sufferers died in their solitude, so that many houses were empty because there had been no one left to take care of the sick; or if they ventured they perished, especially those who aspired to heroism. For they went to see their friends without thought of themselves and were ashamed to leave them, at a time when the very relations of the dying were at last growing weary and ceased even to make lamentations, overwhelmed by the vastness of the calamity. But whatever instances there may have been of such devotion, more often the sick and the dying were tended by the pitying care of those who had recovered, because they knew the course of the disease and were themselves free from apprehension. For no one was ever attacked a second time, or not with a fatal result. All men congratulated them, and they themselves, in the excess of their joy at the moment, had an innocent fancy that they could not die of any other sickness.

The crowding of the people out of the country into the city aggravated the misery; and the newly-arrived suffered most. For, having no houses of their own, but inhabiting in the height of summer stifling huts, the mortality among them was dreadful, and they perished in wild disorder. The dead lay as they had died, one upon another, while others hardly alive wallowed in the streets and crawled about every fountain craving for water. The temples in which they lodged were full of the corpses of those who died in them; for the violence of the calamity was such that men, not knowing where to turn, grew reckless of all law, human and divine. The customs which had hitherto been observed at funerals were universally violated, and they buried their dead each one as best he could. Many, having no proper appliances, because the deaths in their household had been so numerous already, lost all shame in the burial of the dead. When one man had raised a funeral pile, others would come, and throwing on their dead first, set fire to it; or when some other corpse was already burning, before they could be stopped, would throw their own dead upon it and depart.

There were other and worse forms of lawlessness which the plague introduced at Athens. Men who had hitherto concealed what they took pleasure in, now grew bolder. For, seeing the sudden change—how the rich died in a moment, and those who had nothing immediately inherited their property—they reflected that life and riches were alike transitory, and they resolved to enjoy themselves while they could, and to think only of pleasure. Who would be willing to sacrifice himself to the law of honor when he knew not whether he would ever live to be held in honor? The pleasure of the moment and any sort of thing which conduced to it took the place both of honor and of expediency. No fear of Gods or law of man deterred a criminal. Those who saw all perishing alike, thought that the worship or neglect of the Gods made no difference. For offenses against human law no punishment was to be feared; no one would live long enough to be called to account. Already a far heavier sentence had been passed and was hanging over a man's head; before that fell, why should he not take a little pleasure?

What, we may well ask, happens to a people at war, when a third of them are suddenly carried off by some terrible and mysterious force? The suffering and fear caused by the plague must account in part for the rapid descent of a highly civilized people into the depths of cruelty. That awful descent is, in fact, a major theme of Thucydides' *History*. When Pericles died of the plague in 429 B.C., leadership at Athens fell to Cleon, a demagogue from the industrial class. Not much later Athens' important ally on the island of Lesbos, Mytilene, revolted, and to strike terror into the hearts of any allies planning a similar step, the Athenians voted to put to death all the men of Mytilene and to enslave the women and children. They did this on the urging of Cleon. The next day they repented, but with a monstrous cynicism Cleon urged them not to change their minds:

"I have remarked again and again that a democracy cannot manage an empire, but never more than now, when I see you regretting your condemnation of the Mytilenæans. Having no fear or suspicion of one another in daily life, you deal with your allies upon the same principle, and you do not consider that whenever you yield to them out of pity or are misled by their specious tales, you are guilty of a weakness dangerous to yourselves, and receive no thanks from them. You should remember that your empire is a despotism exercised over unwilling subjects, who are always conspiring against you; they do not obey in return for any kindness which you do them to your own injury, but in so far as you are their masters; they have no love of you, but they are held down by force. Besides, what can be more detestable than to be perpetually changing our minds? . . .

"I still maintain that you should abide by your former decision, and not be misled either by pity, or by the charm of words, or by a too forgiving temper. There are no three things more prejudicial to your power. Mercy should be reserved for the merciful, and not thrown away upon those who will have no compassion on us, and who must by the force of circumstances always be our enemies. And our charming orators will still have an arena, but one in which the questions at stake will not be so grave, and the city will not pay so dearly for her brief pleasure in listening to them, while they for a good speech get a good fee. Lastly, forgiveness is naturally shown to those who, being reconciled, will continue friends, and not to those who will always remain what they were, and will abate nothing of their enmity. In one

word, if you do as I say, you will do what is just to
the Mytilenæans, and also what is expedient for yourselves; but, if you take the opposite course, they will
not be grateful to you, and you will be self-con-
demned. For, if they were right in revolting, you
must be wrong in maintaining your empire. But if,
right or wrong, you are resolved to rule, then rightly
or wrongly they must be chastised for your good.
Otherwise you must give up your empire, and, when
virtue is no longer dangerous, you may be as virtuous as you please. Punish them as they would have
punished you."

The Athenians relented, nevertheless, and limited the
death penalty to the leaders of the rebellion, but they did
so on the advice of an orator who could strike no higher
note than this: "The question for us rightly considered
is not, what are the crimes of the Mytilenæans? but, what
is for our interest?" Cleon did his best, however, to keep
the war going, "because he fancied that in the days of
peace his rogueries would be more transparent and his
slanders less credible."

If Periclean imperialism caused the war, says Thucydides, war in turn produced violence, and violence political chaos. With a vivid psychological insight he uses his
description of revolution at Corcyra as an opportunity to
analyze the effect of war on man's character:

When the Corcyræans perceived that the Athenian
fleet was approaching, while that of the enemy had
disappeared, they took the Messenian troops, who
had hitherto been outside the walls, into the city,
and ordered the ships which they had manned to
sail round into the Hyllaic harbor. These proceeded

on their way. Meanwhile they killed any of their enemies whom they caught in the city. On the arrival of the ships they disembarked those whom they had induced to go on board, and dispatched them; they also went to the temple of Hera, and persuading about fifty of the suppliants to stand their trial condemned them all to death. The majority would not come out, and, when they saw what was going on, destroyed one another in the enclosure of the temple where they were, except a few who hung themselves on trees, or put an end to their own lives in any other way which they could. And, during the seven days which Eurymedon after his arrival remained with his sixty ships, the Corcyræans continued slaughtering those of their fellow citizens whom they deemed their enemies; they professed to punish them for their designs against the democracy, but in fact some were killed from motives of personal enmity, and some because money was owing to them, by the hands of their debtors. Every form of death was to be seen; and everything, and more than everything, that commonly happens in revolutions, happened then. The father slew the son, and the suppliants were torn from the temples and slain near them; some of them were even walled up in the temple of Dionysus, and there perished. To such extremes of cruelty did revolution go; and this seemed to be the worst of revolutions, because it was the first.

For not long afterward nearly the whole Hellenic world was in commotion; in every city the chiefs of the democracy and of the oligarchy were struggling, the one to bring in the Athenians, the other the Lacedæmonians. Now in time of peace, men would have had no excuse for introducing either, and no desire to do so; but, when they were at war, the introduction of a foreign alliance on one side or the other to the hurt of their enemies and the advantage of themselves was easily effected by the dissatisfied party. And revolution brought upon the cities of Hellas many terrible calamities, such as have been and always will be while human nature remains the same, but which are more or less aggravated and differ in character with every new combination of circumstances. In peace and prosperity both states and individuals are actuated by higher motives, because they do not fall under the dominion of imperious necessities; but war, which takes away the comfortable provision of daily life, is a hard master and tends to assimilate men's characters to their conditions.

When troubles had once begun in the cities, those who followed carried the revolutionary spirit further and further, and determined to outdo the report of all who had preceded them by the ingenuity of their enterprises and the atrocity of their revenges. The meaning of words had no longer the same relation to things, but was changed by them as they thought proper. Reckless daring was held to be loyal courage; prudent delay was the excuse of a coward; moderation was the disguise of unmanly weakness; to know everything was to do nothing. Frantic energy was the true quality of a man. A conspirator who wanted to be safe was a recreant in disguise. The lover of violence was always trusted, and his opponent suspected. He who succeeded in a plot was deemed knowing, but a still greater master in craft was he who detected one. On the other hand, he who plotted from the first to have nothing to do with plots was a breaker up of parties and a poltroon who was afraid of the enemy. In a word, he who could outstrip another in a bad action was applauded, and so was he who encouraged to evil one who had no idea of it. The tie of party was stronger than the tie of blood, because a partisan was more ready to dare without asking why. (For party associations are not based upon any established law, nor do they seek the public good; they are formed in defiance of the laws and from self-interest.) The seal of good faith was not divine law, but fellowship in crime. If an enemy when he was in the ascendant offered fair words, the opposite party received them not in a generous spirit, but by a jealous watchfulness of his actions. Revenge was dearer than self-preservation. Any agreements sworn to by either party, when they could do nothing else, were binding as long as both were powerless. But he who on a favorable opportunity first took courage, and struck at his enemy when he saw him off his guard, had greater pleasure in a perfidious than he would have had in an open act of revenge; he congratulated himself that he had taken the safer course, and also that he had overreached his enemy and gained the prize of superior ability. In general the dishonest more easily gain credit for cleverness than the simple for goodness; men take a pride in the one, but are ashamed of the other.

The cause of all these evils was the love of power, originating in avarice and ambition, and the party-spirit which is engendered by them when men are fairly embarked in a contest. For the leaders on either side used specious names, the one party professing to uphold the constitutional equality of the many, the other the wisdom of an aristocracy, while they made the public interests, to which in name they were devoted, in reality their prize. Striving in every way to overcome each other, they committed the most monstrous crimes; yet even these were surpassed by the magnitude of their revenges which they pursued to the very utmost, neither party observing any definite limits either of justice or public expediency, but both alike making the caprice of the moment their law. Either by the help of an unrighteous sentence, or grasping power with the strong hand, they were eager to satiate the impatience of party-spirit. Neither faction cared for religion; but any fair pretense which succeeded in effecting some odious purpose was greatly lauded. And the citizens who were of neither party fell a prey to both; either they were disliked because they held aloof, or men were jealous of their surviving.

Thus revolution gave birth to every form of wickedness in Hellas. The simplicity which is so large an element in a noble nature was laughed to scorn and disappeared. An attitude of perfidious antagonism everywhere prevailed; for there was no word binding enough, nor oath terrible enough to reconcile enemies. Each man was strong only in the conviction that nothing was secure; he must look to his own safety, and could not afford to trust others. Inferior intellects generally succeeded best. For, aware of their own deficiencies, and fearing the capacity of their opponents, for whom they were no match in powers of speech, and whose subtle wits were likely to anticipate them in contriving evil, they struck boldly and at once. But the cleverer sort, presuming in their arrogance that they would be aware in time, and disdaining to act when they could think, were taken off their guard and easily destroyed.

And so the war continued until 421 B.C. when, Cleon now dead, an Athenian aristocrat named Nicias brought about a cessation of hostilities. It proved almost impossible, however, to keep the peace because of the reckless ambitions of Alcibiades, the grandnephew and ward of Pericles. Personally charming, but with no moral scruples, Alcibiades saw in war the best way to advance his own

career. Accordingly, he persuaded the Athenians in 416
B. C. to send an expedition against the island of Melos,
which had thus far remained neutral in the war. It was
against this brutal act, which aroused universal hatred of
Athens, that Euripides protested so eloquently the next
year in *The Trojan Women*. Thucydides himself, in his
famous Melian Dialogue, painted the terrifying development by a despotic people of the policy that "might
makes right":

The Athenians next made an expedition against
the island of Melos with thirty ships of their own,
six Chian, and two Lesbian, twelve hundred hoplites
and three hundred archers besides twenty mounted
archers of their own, and about fifteen hundred hoplites furnished by their allies in the islands. The
Melians are colonists of the Lacedæmonians who
would not submit to Athens like the other islanders.
At first they were neutral and took no part. But when
the Athenians tried to coerce them by ravaging their
lands, they were driven into open hostilities. The
generals, Cleomedes the son of Lycomedes and Tisias
the son of Tisimachus, encamped with the Athenian
forces on the island. But before they did the country
any harm they sent envoys to negotiate with the
Melians. Instead of bringing these envoys before the
people, the Melians desired them to explain their
errand to the magistrates and to the dominant class.
They spoke as follows:
"Since we are not allowed to speak to the people,
lest, forsooth, a multitude should be deceived by se-
ductive and unanswerable arguments which they
would hear set forth in a single uninterrupted oration (for we are perfectly aware that this is what you
mean in bringing us before a select few), you who are

sitting here may as well make assurance yet surer. Let us have no set speeches at all, but do you reply to each several statement of which you disapprove, and criticize it at once. Say first of all how you like this mode of proceeding."

The Melian representatives answered: "The quiet interchange of explanations is a reasonable thing, and we do not object to that. But your warlike movements, which are present not only to our fears but to our eyes, seem to belie your words. We see that, although you may reason with us, you mean to be our judges; and that at the end of the discussion, if the justice of our cause prevail and we therefore refuse to yield, we may expect war; if we are convinced by you, slavery."

Athenians: "Nay, but if you are only going to argue from fancies about the future, or if you meet us with any other purpose than that of looking your circumstances in the face and saving your city, we have done; but if this is your intention we will proceed."

Melians: "It is an excusable and natural thing that men in our position should neglect no argument and no view which may avail. But we admit that this conference has met to consider the question of our preservation; and therefore let the argument proceed in the manner which you propose."

Athenians: "Well, then, we Athenians will use no fine words; we will not go out of our way to prove at length that we have a right to rule, because we overthrew the Persians; or that we attack you now because we are suffering any injury at your hands. We should not convince you if we did; nor must you expect to convince us by arguing that, although a colony of the Lacedæmonians, you have taken no part in their expeditions, or that you have never done us any wrong. But you and we should say what we really think, and aim only at what is possible, for we both alike know that into the discussion of human affairs the question of justice only enters where there is equal power to enforce it, and that the powerful exact what they can, and the weak grant what they must."

Melians: "Well, then, since you set aside justice and invite us to speak of expediency, in our judgment it is certainly expedient that you should respect a principle which is for the common good; that to every man when in peril a reasonable claim should be accounted a claim of right, and that any plea which he is disposed to urge, even if failing of the point a little, should help his cause. Your interest in this principle is quite as great as ours, inasmuch as you, if you fall, will incur the heaviest vengeance, and will be the most terrible example to mankind."

Athenians: "The fall of our empire, if it should fall, is not an event to which we look forward with dismay; for ruling states such as Lacedæmon are not cruel to their vanquished enemies. With the Lacedæmonians, however, we are not now contending; the real danger is from our many subject states, who may of their own motion rise up and overcome their masters. But this is a danger which you may leave to us. And we will now endeavor to show that we have come in the interests of our empire, and that in what we are about to say we are only seeking the preservation of your city. For we want to make you ours with the least trouble to ourselves, and it is for the interests of us both that you should not be destroyed."

Melians: "It may be your interest to be our masters, but how can it be ours to be your slaves?"

Athenians: "To you the gain will be that by submission you will avert the worst; and we shall be all the richer for your preservation."

Melians: "But must we be your enemies? Will you not receive us as friends if we are neutral and remain at peace with you?"

Athenians: "No, your enmity is not half so mischievous to us as your friendship; for the one is in the eyes of our subjects an argument of our power, the other of our weakness."

Melians: "But are your subjects really unable to distinguish between states in which you have no concern, and those which are chiefly your own colonies, and in some cases have revolted and been subdued by you?"

Athenians: "Why, they do not doubt that both of them have a good deal to say for themselves on the score of justice, but they think that states like yours are left free because they are able to defend themselves, and that we do not attack them because we dare not. So that your subjection will give us an increase of security, as well as an extension of empire. For we are masters of the sea, and you who are islanders, and insignificant islanders too, must not be allowed to escape us."

Melians: "But do you not recognize another danger? For, once more, since you drive us from the plea of justice and press upon us your doctrine of expediency, we must show you what is for our interest, and, if it be for yours also, may hope to convince you:—Will you not be making enemies of all who are now neutrals? When they see how you are treating us they will expect you some day to turn against them; and if so, are you not strengthening the enemies whom you already have, and bringing upon you others who, if they could help, would never dream of being your enemies at all?"

Athenians: "We do not consider our really dangerous enemies to be any of the peoples inhabiting the mainland who, secure in their freedom, may defer indefinitely any measures of precaution which they take against us, but islanders who, like you, happen to be under no control, and all who may be already irritated by the necessity of submission to our empire—these are our real enemies, for they are the most reckless and most likely to bring themselves as well as us into a danger which they cannot but foresee."

Melians: "Surely then, if you and your subjects will brave all this risk, you to preserve your empire and they to be quit of it, how base and cowardly would it be in us, who retain our freedom, not to do and suffer anything rather than be your slaves."

Athenians: "Not so, if you calmly reflect: for you are not fighting against equals to whom you cannot yield without disgrace, but you are taking counsel whether or no you shall resist an overwhelming force. The question is not one of honor but of prudence."

Melians: "But we know that the fortune of war is sometimes impartial, and not always on the side of numbers. If we yield now, all is over; but if we fight, there is yet a hope that we may stand upright."

Athenians: "Hope is a good comforter in the hour of danger, and when men have something else to depend upon, although hurtful, she is not ruinous. But when her spendthrift nature has induced them to stake their all, they see her as she is in the moment of their fall, and not till then. While the knowledge of her might enable them to beware of her, she never fails. You are weak and a single turn of the scale might be your ruin. Do not you be thus deluded; avoid the error of which so many are guilty, who, although they might still be saved if they would take the natural means, when visible grounds of confidence forsake them, have recourse to the invisible, to prophecies and oracles and the like, which ruin men by the hopes which they inspire in them."

Melians: "We know only too well how hard the struggle must be against your power, and against fortune, if she does not mean to be impartial. Nevertheless we do not despair of fortune; for we hope to stand as high as you in the favor of heaven, because we are righteous, and you against whom we contend are unrighteous; and we are satisfied that our deficiency in power will be compensated by the aid of our allies the Lacedæmonians; they cannot refuse to help us, if only because we are their kinsmen, and for the sake of their own honor. And therefore our confidence is not so utterly blind as you suppose."

Athenians: "As for the Gods, we expect to have quite as much of their favor as you: for we are not doing or claiming anything which goes beyond common opinion about divine or men's desires about human things. For of the Gods we believe, and of men we know, that by a law of their nature wherever they can rule they will. This law was not made by us, and we are not the first who have acted upon it; we did but inherit it, and shall bequeath it to all time, and we know that you and all mankind, if you were as strong as we are, would do as we do. So much for the Gods; we have told you why we expect to stand as high in their good opinion as you. And then as to the Lacedæmonians—when you imagine that out of very shame they will assist you, we admire the innocence of your idea, but we do not envy you the folly of it. The Lacedæmonians are exceedingly virtuous among themselves, and according to their national standard of morality. But, in respect of their dealings with others, although many things might be said, they can be described in few words—of all men whom we know they are the most notorious for identifying what is pleasant with what is honorable, and what is expedient with what is just. But how inconsistent is such a character with your present blind hope of deliverance!"

Melians: "That is the very reason why we trust them; they will look to their interest, and therefore will not be willing to betray the Melians, who are their own colonists, lest they should be distrusted by their friends in Hellas and play into the hands of their enemies."

Athenians: "But do you not see that the path of expediency is safe, whereas justice and honor involve danger in practice, and such dangers the Lacedæmonians seldom care to face?"

Melians: "On the other hand, we think that whatever perils there may be, they will be ready to face them for our sakes, and will consider danger less dangerous where we are concerned. For if they need our aid we are close at hand, and they can better trust our loyal feeling because we are their kinsmen."

Athenians: "Yes, but what encourages men who are invited to join in a conflict is clearly not the good will of those who summon them to their side, but a decided superiority in real power. To this no men look more keenly than the Lacedæmonians; so little confidence have they in their own resources, that they only attack their neighbors when they have numerous allies, and therefore they are not likely to find their way by themselves to an island, when we are masters of the sea."

Melians: "But they may send their allies: the Cretan sea is a large place; and the masters of the sea will have more difficulty in overtaking vessels which want to escape than the pursued in escaping. If the attempt should fail they may invade Attica itself, and find their way to allies of yours whom Brasidas did not reach: and then you will have to fight, not for the conquest of a land in which you have no concern, but nearer home, for the preservation of your confederacy and of your own territory."

Athenians: "Help may come from Lacedæmon to you as it has come to others, and should you ever have actual experience of it, then you will know that never once have the Athenians retired from a siege through fear of a foe elsewhere. You told us that the safety of your city would be your first care, but we remark that, in this long discussion, not a word has been uttered by you which would give a reasonable man expectation of deliverance. Your strongest grounds are hopes deferred, and what power you have is not to be compared with that which is already arrayed against you. Unless after we have withdrawn you mean to come, as even now you may, to a wiser conclusion, you are showing a great want of sense. For surely you cannot dream of flying to that false sense of honor which has been the ruin of so many when danger and dishonor were staring them in the face. Many men with their eyes still open to the consequences have found the word 'honor' too much for them, and have suffered a mere name to lure them on, until it has drawn down upon them real and irretrievable calamities; through their own folly they have incurred a worse dishonor than fortune would have inflicted upon them. If you are wise you will not run this risk; you ought to see that there can be no disgrace in yielding to a great city which invites you to become her ally on reasonable terms, keeping your own land, and merely paying tribute; and that you will certainly gain no honor if, having to choose between two alternatives, safety and war, you obstinately prefer the worse. To maintain our rights against equals, to be politic with superiors, and to be moderate toward inferiors is the path of safety. Reflect once more when we have withdrawn, and say to yourselves over and over again that you are deliberating about your one and only country, which may be saved or may be destroyed by a single de-cision."

The Athenians left the conference: the Melians, after consulting among themselves, resolved to per-severe in their refusal, and made answer as follows: "Men of Athens, our resolution is unchanged; and we will not in a moment surrender that liberty which our city, founded seven hundred years ago, still en-joys; we will trust to the good fortune which, by the favor of the Gods, has hitherto preserved us, and for human help to the Lacedæmonians, and endeavor to save ourselves. We are ready however to be your friends, and the enemies neither of you nor of the Lacedæmonians, and we ask you to leave our country when you have made such a peace as may appear to be in the interest of both parties."

Such was the answer of the Melians; the Athenians, as they quitted the conference, spoke as follows: "Well, we must say, judging from the decision at which you have arrived, that you are the only men who deem the future to be more certain than the present, and regard things unseen as already realized in your fond anticipation, and that the more you cast yourselves upon the Lacedæmonians and fortune and hope, and trust them, the more complete will be your ruin."

The Athenian envoys returned to the army; and the generals, when they found that the Melians would not yield, immediately commenced hostilities. They surrounded the town of Melos with a wall, dividing the work among the several contingents. They then left troops of their own and of their allies to keep guard both by land and by sea, and retired with the greater part of their army; the remainder carried on the blockade.

The Melians took that part of the Athenian wall

which looked toward the Agora by a night assault, killed a few men, and brought in as much grain and other necessaries as they could; they then retreated and remained inactive. After this the Athenians set a better watch.

About the same time the Melians took another part of the Athenian wall; for the fortifications were insufficiently guarded. Whereupon the Athenians sent fresh troops, under the command of Philocrates the son of Demeas. The place was now closely invested, and there was treachery among the citizens themselves. So the Melians were induced to surrender at discretion. The Athenians thereupon put to death all who were of military age, and made slaves of the women and children. They then colonized the island, sending thither five hundred settlers of their own.

The excitement of military service, the eagerness to do almost anything, even to go to war, to escape from the humdrum routine of ordinary life, the hope of older men for a command and of the younger for the joy of adventure, with a pot of gold at the end of the rainbow for all—these were some of the motives back of Athens' support of the next imperialistic folly, the unprovoked attack on Corinth's great colony in Sicily, Syracuse (415–413 B.C.). Emboldened by his successful venture at Melos, Alcibiades now urged the Athenians to embark on the western expedition. Eventually two glorious fleets sailed from Athens, with 45,000 Athenians and their allies, few of whom ever returned home. Nicias had opposed Alcibiades and had tried to dissuade the people by showing the numbers of men and ships that would be needed, but it was no use:

Far from losing their enthusiasm at the disagreeable prospect, the Athenians were more determined than ever; they approved of his advice, and were confident that every chance of danger was now removed. All alike were seized with a passionate desire to sail, the elder among them convinced that they would achieve the conquest of Sicily—at any rate such an armament could suffer no disaster; the youth were longing to see with their own eyes the marvels of a distant land, and were confident of a safe return; the main body of the troops expected to receive present pay, and to conquer a country which would be an inexhaustible mine of pay for the future. The enthusiasm of the majority was so overwhelming that, although some disapproved, they were afraid of being thought unpatriotic if they voted on the other side, and therefore held their peace. . . .

The city had newly recovered from the plague and from the constant pressure of war; a new population had grown up; there had been time for the accumulation of money during the peace; so that there was abundance of everything at command. . . .

About the middle of summer the expedition started for Sicily. Orders had been previously given to most of the allies, to the grain-ships, the smaller craft, and generally to the vessels in attendance on the armament, that they should muster at Corcyra, whence the whole fleet was to strike across the Ionian Gulf to the promontory of Iapygia. Early in the morning of the day appointed for their departure, the Athenian forces and such of their allies as had already joined them went down to Piræus and began to man the ships. Almost the entire population of Athens accompanied them, citizens and strangers alike. The citizens came to take farewell, one of an acquaintance, another of a kinsman, another of a son, and as they passed along were full of hope and full of tears; hope of conquering Sicily, tears because they doubted whether they would ever see their friends again, when they thought of the long voyage on which they were going away. At the last moment of parting the danger was nearer; and terrors which had never occurred to them when they were voting the expedition now entered into their souls. Nevertheless their spirit revived at the sight of the armament in all its strength and of the abundant provision which they had made. The strangers and the rest of the multitude came out of curiosity, desiring to witness an enterprise of which the greatness exceeded belief.

No armament so magnificent or costly had ever been sent out by any single Hellenic power, though in mere number of ships and hoplites that which sailed to Epidaurus under Pericles and afterward under Hagnon to Potidæa was not inferior. For that expedition consisted of a hundred Athenian and fifty Chian and Lesbian triremes, conveying four thousand hoplites, all Athenian citizens, three hundred cavalry, and a multitude of allied troops. Still the voyage was short and the equipments were poor, whereas this expedition was intended to be long absent, and was thoroughly provided both for sea and land service, wherever its presence might be required. On the fleet the greatest pains and expense had been lavished by the trierarchs and the state. The public treasury gave a drachma a day to each sailor, and furnished empty hulls for sixty swift-sailing vessels, and for forty transports carrying hoplites. All these were manned with the best crews which could be obtained. The trierarchs, besides the pay given by the state, added somewhat more out of their own means to the wages of the upper ranks of rowers and of the petty officers. The figure-heads and other fittings provided by them were of the most costly description. Every one strove to the utmost that his own ship might excel both in

beauty and swiftness. The infantry had been well
selected and the lists carefully made up. There was
the keenest rivalry among the soldiers in the matter
of arms and personal equipment. And while at home
the Athenians were thus competing with one another
in the performance of their several duties, to the rest
of Hellas the expedition seemed to be a grand dis-
play of their power and greatness, rather than a preparation for war. If anyone had reckoned up the whole
expenditure, both of the state and of individual soldiers and others, including in the first not only what
the city had already laid out, but what was entrusted
to the generals, and in the second what either at the
time or afterward private persons spent upon their
outfit, or the trierarchs upon their ships, the provision for the long voyage which every one may be
supposed to have carried with him over and above his
public pay, and what soldiers or traders may have
taken for purposes of exchange, he would have found
that altogether an immense sum amounting to many
talents was withdrawn from the city. Men were quite
amazed at the boldness of the scheme and the magnificence of the spectacle, which were everywhere
spoken of, no less than at the great disproportion of
the force when compared with that of the enemy
against whom it was intended. Never had a greater
expedition been sent to a foreign land; never was
there an enterprise in which the hope of future success
seemed to be better justified by actual power.

When the ships were manned and everything required for the voyage had been placed on board,
silence was proclaimed by the sound of the trumpet,
and all with one voice before setting sail offered up
the customary prayers; these were recited, not in each
ship separately, but by a single herald, the whole fleet
accompanying him. On every deck both the officers

and the marines, mingling wine in bowls, made libations from vessels of gold and silver. The multitude of citizens and other well-wishers who were looking on from the land joined in the prayer. The crews raised the pæan and, when the libations were completed, put to sea. After sailing out for some distance in single file, the ships raced with one another as far as Ægina; thence they hastened onward to Corcyra, where the allies who formed the rest of the army were assembling.

Athens lost her long war with Sparta, Thucydides believed, because the people followed the urgings of self-seeking demagogues, who pandered to the basest instincts of the masses. Against the advice of Pericles the Athenians persisted in further conquest while the war continued and were ever ready to engage in intense party warfare. Nothing more unfortunate could be imagined than their choice of generals for the Sicilian expedition: Nicias, who had opposed it from the start; Lamachus, a stolid fighter of the old school, who was killed soon after reaching Sicily; and Alcibiades, who was recalled early in the expedition and immediately deserted to Sparta.

So many disasters fell on the Athenians before Syracuse that finally they had no alternative but to try to force their way out of the harbor and flee back to Athens. As Thucydides describes the concluding events of the ill-starred expedition, we are caught up in a great tragedy:

Many vessels meeting—and never did so many fight in so small a space, for the two fleets together amounted to nearly two hundred—they were seldom able to strike in the regular manner, because they had no opportunity of first retiring or breaking the line; they generally fouled one another as ship dashed against ship in the hurry of flight or pursuit. All the time that another vessel was bearing down, the men on deck poured showers of javelins and arrows and stones upon the enemy; and when the two closed, the marines fought hand to hand, and endeavored to board. In many places, owing to the want of room, they who had struck another found that they were struck themselves; often two or even more vessels were unavoidably entangled about one, and the pilots had to make plans of attack and defense, not against one adversary only, but against several coming from different sides. The crash of so many ships dashing against one another took away the wits of the crews, and made it impossible to hear the boatswains, whose voices in both fleets rose high, as they gave directions to the rowers, or cheered them on in the excitement of the struggle. On the Athenian side they were shouting to their men that they must force a passage and seize the opportunity now or never of returning in safety to their native land. To the Syracusans and their allies was represented the glory of preventing the escape of their enemies, and of a victory by which every man would exalt the honor of his own city. The commanders too, when they saw any ship backing without necessity, would call the captain by his name, and ask, of the Athenians, whether they were retreating because they expected to be more at home upon the land of their bitterest foes than upon that sea which had been their own so long; on the Syracusan side, whether, when they knew perfectly well that the Athenians were only eager to find some means of flight, they would themselves fly from the fugitives.

While the naval engagement hung in the balance the two armies on shore had great trial and conflict of soul. The Sicilian soldier was animated by the hope of increasing the glory which he had already won, while the invader was tormented by the fear that his fortunes might sink lower still. The last chance of the Athenians lay in their ships, and their anxiety was dreadful. The fortune of the battle varied; and it was not possible that the spectators on the shore should all receive the same impression of it. Being quite close and having different points of view, they would some of them see their own ships victorious; their courage would then revive, and they would earnestly call upon the Gods not to take from them their hope of deliverance. But others, who saw their ships worsted, cried and shrieked aloud, and were by the sight alone more utterly unnerved than the defeated combatants themselves. Others again, who had fixed their gaze on some part of the struggle which was undecided, were in a state of excitement still more terrible; they kept swaying their bodies to and fro in an agony of hope and fear as the stubborn conflict went on and on; for at every instant they were all but saved or all but lost. And while the strife hung in the balance you might hear in the Athenian army at once lamentation, shouting, cries of victory or defeat, and all the various sounds which are wrung from a great host in extremity of danger. Not less agonizing were the feelings of those on board. At length the Syracusans and their allies, after a protracted struggle, put the Athenians to flight, and triumphantly bearing down upon them, and encouraging one another with loud cries and exhortations, drove them to land. Then that part of the navy which had not been taken in the deep water fell back in confusion to the shore, and the crews rushed out of the ships into the camp. And the land-forces, no longer now divided in feeling, but uttering one universal groan of intolerable anguish, ran, some of them to save the ships, others to defend what remained of the wall; but the greater number began to look to themselves and to their own safety. Never had there been a greater panic in an Athenian army than at that moment. They now suffered what they had done to others at Pylos. For at Pylos the Lacedæmonians, when they saw their ships destroyed, knew that their friends who had crossed over into the island of Sphacteria were lost with them. And so now the Athenians, after the rout of their fleet, knew that they had no hope of saving themselves by land unless events took some extraordinary turn.

Their fleet destroyed, nothing remained for the Athenians except retreat by land and, as it happened, ultimate surrender:

On the third day after the sea-fight, when Nicias and Demosthenes thought that their preparations were complete, the army began to move. They were in a dreadful condition; not only was there the great fact that they had lost their whole fleet, and instead of their expected triumph had brought the utmost peril upon Athens as well as upon themselves, but also the sights which presented themselves as they quitted the camp were painful to every eye and mind. The dead were unburied, and when any one saw the body of a friend lying on the ground he was smitten with sorrow and dread, while the sick or wounded who still survived but had to be left were even a greater trial to the living, and more to be pitied than those who were gone. Their prayers and lamentations drove their companions to distraction; they would beg that they might be taken with them, and call by name any friend or relation whom they saw passing; they would hang upon their departing comrades and follow as far as they could, and, when their limbs and strength failed them, and they dropped behind, many were the imprecations and cries which they uttered. So that the whole army was in tears, and such was their despair that they could hardly make up their minds to stir, although they were leaving an enemy's country, having suffered calamities too great for tears already, and dreading miseries yet greater in the unknown future.

There was also a general feeling of shame and self-reproach—indeed they seemed, not like an army, but like the fugitive population of a city captured after a siege; and of a great city too. For the whole multitude who were marching together numbered not less than forty thousand. Each of them took with him anything he could carry which was likely to be of use. Even the heavy-armed and cavalry, contrary to their practice when under arms, conveyed about their persons their own food, some because they had no attendants, others because they could not trust them; for they had long been deserting, and most of them had gone off all at once. Nor was the food which they carried sufficient; for the supplies of the camp had failed. Their disgrace and the universality of the misery, although there might be some consolation in the very community of suffering, were nevertheless at that moment hard to bear, especially when they remembered from what pride and splendor they had fallen into their present low estate. Never had an Hellenic army experienced such a reverse. They had come intending to enslave others, and they were going away in fear that they would be themselves enslaved. Instead of the prayers and hymns with which they had put to sea, they were now departing amid appeals to heaven of another sort. They were no longer sailors but landsmen, depending, not upon their fleet, but upon their infantry. Yet in face of the great danger which still threatened them all these things appeared endurable. . . .

When the day dawned Nicias led forward his army, and the Syracusans and the allies again assailed them on every side, hurling javelins and other missiles at them. The Athenians hurried on to the river Assinarus. They hoped to gain a little relief if they forded the river, for the mass of horsemen and other troops overwhelmed and crushed them; and they were worn out by fatigue and thirst. But no sooner did they reach the water than they lost all order and rushed in; every man was trying to cross first, and, the enemy pressing upon them at the same time, the passage of the river became hopeless. Being compelled to keep close together they fell one upon another, and trampled each other under foot: some at once perished, pierced by their own spears; others got entangled in the baggage and were carried down the stream. The Syracusans stood upon the further bank of the river, which was steep, and hurled missiles from above on the Athenians, who were huddled together in the deep bed of the stream and for the most part were drinking greedily. The Peloponnesians came down the bank and slaughtered them, falling chiefly upon those who were in the river. Whereupon the water at once became foul, but was drunk all the same, although muddy and dyed with blood, and the crowd fought for it.

At last, when the dead bodies were lying in heaps upon one another in the water and the army was utterly undone, some perishing in the river, and any who escaped being cut off by the cavalry, Nicias surrendered to Gylippus, in whom he had more confidence than in the Syracusans. He entreated him and the Lacedæmonians to do what they pleased with himself, but not to go on killing the men. So Gylippus gave the word to make prisoners. . . .

Those who were imprisoned in the quarries were at the beginning of their captivity harshly treated by the Syracusans. There were great numbers of them, and they were crowded in a deep and narrow place. At first the sun by day was still scorching and suffocating, for they had no roof over their heads, while the autumn nights were cold, and the extremes of temperature engendered violent disorders. Being cramped for room they had to do everything on the same spot. The corpses of those who died from their wounds, exposure to heat and cold, and the like, lay heaped one upon another. The smells were intolerable; and they were at the same time afflicted by hunger and thirst. During eight months they were allowed only about half a pint of water and a pint of food a day. Every kind of misery which could befall man in such a place befell them. This was the condition of all the captives for about ten weeks. At length the Syracusans sold them, with the exception of the Athenians and of any Sicilian or Italian Greeks who had sided with them in the war. The whole number of the public prisoners is not accurately known, but they were not less than seven thousand.

Of all the Hellenic actions which took place in this war, or indeed, as I think, of all Hellenic actions which are on record, this was the greatest—the most glorious to the victors, the most ruinous to the vanquished; for they were utterly and at all points defeated, and their sufferings were prodigious. Fleet and army perished from the face of the earth; nothing was saved, and of the many who went forth few returned home.

Thus ended the Sicilian expedition.

The resilience of the Athenians after the Sicilian disaster seems downright incredible. For nine more years they persisted, they raised new fleets and with an elastic spirit turned down Spartan offers of peace. The victorious Syracusan fleet appeared on the Ægean, the Persian king promised military and financial aid, Athenian allies revolted, there was a brief oligarchical revolution in Athens itself, and yet the people kept on. Thanks to the advice of Alcibiades, Sparta now maintained a permanent garrison in Attica, so that the Athenians were crowded into the city throughout the year and not, as previously, merely during the campaigning summer months. Suffering increased, the supplies of food ran low, and the financial resources of the state were practically exhausted.

Thucydides outlived the Peloponnesian War by several years, but he died before he could finish his *History*. For the fall of Athens, therefore, we are dependent on another Athenian historian, Xenophon. He has left us a moving description of the last days of the imperial democracy, when the state trireme *Paralus* reached Piræus with the news that the last possible Athenian fleet with the last available crews had been destroyed in battle:

It was night when the *Paralus* reached Athens with her evil tidings, on receipt of which a bitter wail of woe broke forth. From Piræus, following the line of the Long Walls up to the heart of the city, it swept and swelled, as each man to his neighbor passed on the news. On that night no man slept. There was mourning and sorrow for those that were lost, but the lamentation for the dead was merged in even deeper sorrow for themselves, as they pictured the evils they were about to suffer, the like of which they had themselves inflicted upon the men of Melos, who were colonists of the Lacedæmonians, when they mastered them by siege. Or on the men of Histiæa; on Scione and Torone; on the Æginetans, and many another Hellenic city. On the following day the public assembly met, and, after debate, it was resolved to block up all the harbors save one, to put the walls in a state of defense, to post guards at various points, and to make all other necessary preparation for a siege. Such were the concerns of the men of Athens. . . .

The Athenians, finding themselves besieged by land and sea, were in sore perplexity what to do. Without ships, without allies, without provisions, the belief gained hold upon them that there was no way of escape. They must now, in their turn, suffer what they had themselves inflicted upon others; not in retaliation, indeed, for ills received, but out of sheer insolence, overriding the citizens of petty states, and for no better reason than that these were allies of the very men now at the gates. In this frame of mind they enfranchised those who at any time had lost their civil rights, and schooled themselves to endurance; and, albeit many succumbed to starvation, no thought of truce or reconciliation with their foes was breathed. But when the stock of grain was absolutely insufficient, they sent an embassy to Agis, proposing to become allies of the Lacedæmonians on the sole condition of keeping their fortification walls and Piræus; and to draw up articles of treaty on these terms. Agis bade them betake themselves to Lacedæmon, seeing that he had no authority to act himself. With this answer the ambassadors returned to Athens, and were forthwith sent on to Lacedæmon. On reaching Sellasia, a town in Laconian territory, they waited till they got their answer from the ephors, who, having learnt their terms (which were identical with those already proposed to Agis), bade them instantly to be gone, and, if they really desired peace, to come with other proposals, the fruit of happier reflection. Thus the ambassadors returned home, and reported the result of their embassy, whereupon despondency fell upon all. It was a painful reflection that in the end they would be sold into slavery; and meanwhile, pending the return of a second embassy, many must needs fall victims to starvation. The razing of their fortifications was not a solution which any one cared to recommend. A person, Archestratus, had indeed put the question in the Council, whether it were not best to make peace with the Lacedæmonians on such terms as they were willing to propose; but he was thrown into prison. The Laconian proposals referred to involved the destruction of both Long Walls for a space of more than a mile. And a decree had been passed, making it illegal to submit any such proposition about the walls. Things having reached this pass, Theramenes made a proposal in the public assembly as follows: If they chose to send him as an ambassador to Lysander, he would go and find out why the Lacedæmonians were so unyielding about the walls; whether it was they really intended to enslave the city, or merely that they wanted a guarantee of good faith. Dispatched accordingly, he lingered on with Lysander for three whole months and more, watching for the time when the Athenians, at the last pinch of starvation, would be willing to accede to any terms that might be offered. . . .

Theramenes and his companions presently reached Sellasia, and being here questioned as to the reason of their visit, replied that they had full powers to treat of peace. After which the ephors ordered them to be summoned to their presence. On their arrival a general assembly was convened, in which the Corinthians and Thebans more particularly, though their views were shared by many other Hellenes also, urged the meeting not to come to terms with the Athenians, but to destroy them. The Lacedæmonians replied that they would never reduce to slavery a city which was itself an integral portion of Hellas, and had performed a great and noble service to Hellas in the most perilous of emergencies. On the contrary, they were willing to offer peace on the terms now specified—namely, "That the Long Walls and the fortifications of Piræus should be destroyed; that the Athenian fleet, with the exception of twelve vessels, should be surrendered; that the exiles should be restored; and lastly, that the Athenians should acknowledge the headship of Sparta in peace and war, leaving to her the choice of friends and foes, and following her lead by land and sea." Such were the terms which Theramenes and the rest who acted with him were able to report on their return to Athens. As they entered the city, a vast crowd met them, trembling lest their mission should have proved fruitless. For indeed delay was no longer possible, so long already was the list of victims daily perishing from starvation. On the day following, the ambassadors delivered their report, stating the terms upon which the Lacedæmonians were willing to make peace. Theramenes acted as spokesman, insisting that they ought to obey the Lacedæmonians and pull down the walls. A small minority raised their voice in opposition, but the majority were strongly in favor of the proposition, and the resolution was passed to accept the peace. After that, Lysander sailed into Piræus, and the exiles were re-admitted. And so they fell to leveling the fortifications and walls with much enthusiasm, to the accompaniment of female flute players, deeming that day the beginning of liberty to Greece.

And so, indeed, the new day dawned, with flute players celebrating the beginning of liberty in Greece as the walls of a great democracy came down. Words had lost their meaning, and so had much else in Greek civilization.

VII

THE FUTURE

IN HIS PROVOCATIVE BOOK, *The World and the West,* Arnold Toynbee addresses himself to the contribution that antiquity can make to an understanding of our own future. If we would peer into the unfinished history of tomorrow, he says, we must "turn to the history of the world's encounter with the Greeks and Romans; for, in the record of this episode, the scroll of history has already been unrolled from beginning to end, so that the whole of this older book now lies open for our inspection. Our future can perhaps be deciphered in this record of a Græco–Roman past." This puts us in mind of Lord Acton's famous injunction, that "the prize of all history is the understanding of modern times."

Toynbee went on to point out that, after the Romans had conquered the East, there came from the East a counteroffensive, that of religion, which in turn conquered the West. Some reviewers thought that Toynbee was suggesting that once again from the East, now conquered technologically by the West, there would come a conquering force, that of Communism. But Toynbee rejected this vigorously in a letter to the *London Times Literary Supplement* for April 16, 1954, and added the following clarification of his ideas on the future:

"I guess that the West is going to be converted to some religion which, like Mahayanian Buddhism, Mithraism and Christianity, calls on us to worship a god who is not a deification of our human selves. . . . I guess that both the West and the world are going to turn away from man-worshipping ideologies—Communism and secular individualism alike—and become converted to an Oriental religion coming neither from Russia nor from the West. I guess that this will be the Christian religion that came to the Greeks and Romans from Palestine, with one of two elements in traditional Christianity discarded and replaced by a new element from India. I expect and hope that this avatar of Christianity will include the vision of God as being Love. But I also expect and hope that it will discard the other traditional Christian vision of God as being a jealous god, and that it will reject the self-glorification of this jealous god's 'Chosen People' as being unique. This is where India comes in, with her belief (complementary to the vision of God as Love) that there may be more than one illuminating and saving approach to the mystery of the universe."

It is an interesting, if easy, parallel. To be sure, a religion that becomes universally adopted and displaces the state that nurtured it is a very real phenomenon and represents one of the few decisive and permanent changes in the history of man. Actually, however, the question is not whether some new force is about to conquer us, as Christianity once supplanted ancient civilization, but rather how it came about that ancient man eventually decided to substitute one attitude toward the world for another. The reasons for desiring a change come before the change itself: such reasons may remain constant and thus are of contemporary significance, whereas the form the change takes may vary from period to period.

It is a startling fact that each of the politically dominant people of antiquity, the Greeks and the Romans, should first win at least a theoretical or potential democracy, then lose faith in it, and finally succumb to one-man rule. At the end of the Greek triumph—especially that of Athens —stands Alexander the Great; at the end of the Roman, Augustus. If we could say why faith in the possibilities of democracy was won and lost, not once but twice and forever afterward in antiquity, we would probably have the secret of history's most important lesson.

It is ironical to observe that Rome's "glorious" victory over Hannibal produced a series of almost insoluble problems. The crisis of the long war, with the citizens absent in the armies, meant that the Senate more and more usurped the sole right to rule. When the war ended, and Rome continued to round out her domain successfully, there was a disposition on the part of ordinary citizens to let the Senate remain at the helm. Could the march toward democracy be resumed, how were new foreign influences (especially the sophisticated Greek) to be regarded, what means were to be devised for governing the newly acquired provinces, what was to be done about the growing urban population, composed chiefly of small farmers who had been ruined by Hannibal's devastation? Toward the end of the second century B.C. two brothers, Tiberius and Gaius Gracchus, tried to solve these problems, but when the reactionary senatorial class blocked their efforts, the ancient world was caught up in terrible conflict. The century-long Roman Revolution, which had begun in the interest of the city masses, ended with the fall of the republic, the establishment of the empire, and the survival of the aristocracy as the dominant class. Does intense party strife produce despair and desire for change, chaos, and the loss of civil liberty?

The Greeks, paced by Athens, had already passed

through much the same experience. Liberality bore the twin fruits of democracy and greatness, but when the disappointed, selfish masses were denied full partnership in the developing culture, avaricious leaders were able to drive them to excesses. Party strife, war, despair, and one-man rule followed. The revolutions at Athens and Rome were different in kind, however. The Athenian was a class struggle that tended to bring the riff-raff to the top—which provides its own commentary on the extent of Pericles' success—whereas the conflict at Rome was between aristocractic factions.

There were many reasons why Athens lost the war with Sparta. Party strife, the selfish greed and excesses of the masses, and unscrupulous demagogues stand high on Thucydides' list. But it is equally certain that the Peloponnesian War harmed the victorious almost as much as the vanquished. Despite the great thinkers, such as Plato, who flourished in the next century, individualism and narrow group loyalties began to supplant the traditional devotion to the state. Perhaps this was inevitable because, with the disappearance of the Athenian Empire and its promise of stability, men considered it sensible to think primarily of themselves and the class to which they belonged.

In a sense the fourth century B.C. presents the picture of a society in disintegration, where class feeling and despair, envy of the other man's riches, and the withdrawal of cultivated citizens from political life seem the chief characteristics of the new day. But as faith in the city-state declined, hope of a larger state system, one in which man might move on the level of world rather than regional politics, took its place.

Certain Greek thinkers, for example, thought it a pity

that their countrymen did not make war upon a common
foe instead of continuing their fratricidal strife. Still
others believed simply that the cure of all their troubles
lay in monarchy. The two ideas fused in popular thought,
and there thus grew up in the Greek world a conviction
that the Greeks should unite under a king and make war
against a common enemy. It was in precisely this fashion
that the fourth century ended, for the Greeks were united
forcibly under the Macedonian king, Alexander, in a war
against Persia. To be sure, Alexander gave a tremendous
impetus to Greek civilization, but henceforth its development was along lines very different from those of Periclean
Athens.

As Plato, from his vantage point of the complex fourth
century with all its contradictions, looked back on the fall
of Athens and more especially on the problems of man, he
challenged men of whatever era to seek philosophical en-
lightenment, if they hoped to achieve the good life and
avoid disaster in their own time. In the famous parable of
the Cave, from the seventh book of the *Republic,* Socrates
is speaking with Glaucon:

And now, I said, let me show in a figure how far
our nature is enlightened or unenlightened:—Behold! human beings living in an underground cave,
which has a mouth open towards the light and reaching all along the cave; here they have been from their
childhood, and have their legs and necks chained so
that they cannot move, and can only see before them,
being prevented by the chains from turning round
their heads. Above and behind them a fire is blazing
at a distance, and between the fire and the prisoners
there is a raised way; and you will see, if you look, a

low wall built along the way, like the screen which marionette players have in front of them, over which they show the puppets.

I see.

And do you see, I said, men passing along the wall carrying all sorts of vessels, and statues and figures of animals made of wood and stone and various materials, which appear over the wall? Some of them are talking, others silent.

You have shown me a strange image, and they are strange prisoners.

Like ourselves, I replied; and they see only their own shadows, or the shadows of one another, which the fire throws on the opposite wall of the cave?

True, he said; how could they see anything but the shadows if they were never allowed to move their heads?

And of the objects which are being carried in like manner they would only see the shadows?

Yes, he said.

And if they were able to converse with one another, would they not suppose that they were naming what was actually before them?

Very true.

And suppose further that the prison had an echo which came from the other side, would they not be sure to fancy when one of the passers-by spoke that the voice which they heard came from the passing shadow?

No question, he replied.

To them, I said, the truth would be literally nothing but the shadows of the images.

That is certain.

And now look again, and see what will naturally follow if the prisoners are released and disabused of their error. At first, when any of them is liberated and compelled suddenly to stand up and turn his neck round and walk and look toward the light, he will suffer sharp pains; the glare will distress him, and he will be unable to see the realities of which in his former state he had seen the shadows; and then conceive some one saying to him, that what he saw before was an illusion, but that now, when he is approaching nearer to being and his eye is turned towards more real existence, he has a clearer vision—what will be his reply? And you may further imagine that his instructor is pointing to the objects as they pass and requiring him to name them—will he not be perplexed? Will he not fancy that the shadows which he formerly saw are truer than the objects which are now shown to him?

Far truer.

And if he is compelled to look straight at the light, will he not have a pain in his eyes which will make him turn away to take refuge in the objects of vision which he can see, and which he will conceive to be in reality clearer than the things which are now being shown to him?

True, he said.

And suppose once more, that he is reluctantly dragged up a steep and rugged ascent, and held fast until he is forced into the presence of the sun himself, is he not likely to be pained and irritated? When he approaches the light his eyes will be dazzled, and he will not be able to see anything at all of what are now called realities.

Not all in a moment, he said.

He will require to grow accustomed to the sight of the upper world. And first he will see the shadows best, next the reflections of men and other objects in the water, and then the objects themselves; then he will gaze upon the light of the moon and the stars and the spangled heaven; and he will see the sky and the stars by night better than the sun or the light of the sun by day?

Certainly.

Last of all he will be able to see the sun, and not mere reflections of him in the water, but he will see him in his own proper place, and not in another; and he will contemplate him as he is.

Certainly.

He will then proceed to argue that this is he who gives the season and the years, and is the guardian of all that is in the visible world, and in a certain way the cause of all things which he and his fellows have been accustomed to behold?

Clearly, he said, he would first see the sun and then reason about him.

And when he remembered his old habitation, and the wisdom of the cave and his fellow-prisoners, do you not suppose that he would felicitate himself on the change, and pity them?

Certainly, he would.

And if they were in the habit of conferring honors among themselves on those who were quickest to observe the passing shadows and to remark which of them went before, and which followed after, and which were together; and who were therefore best able to draw conclusions as to the future, do you think that he would care for such honors and glories, or envy the possessors of them? Would he not say with Homer,

'Better to be the poor servant of a poor master,' and to endure anything, rather than think as they do and live after their manner?

Yes, he said, I think that he would rather suffer anything than entertain these false notions and live in this miserable manner.

Imagine once more, I said, such an one coming suddenly out of the sun to be replaced in his old situation; would he not be certain to have his eyes full of darkness?

To be sure, he said.

And if there were a contest, and he had to compete in measuring the shadows with the prisoners who had never moved out of the cave, while his sight was still weak, and before his eyes had become steady (and the time which would be needed to acquire this new habit of sight might be very considerable), would he not be ridiculous? Men would say of him that up he went and down he came without his eyes; and that it was better not even to think of ascending; and if any one tried to loose another and lead him up to the light, let them only catch the offender, and they would put him to death.

No question, he said.

This entire allegory, I said, you may now append, dear Glaucon, to the previous argument; the prison-house is the world of sight, the light of the fire is the sun, and you will not misapprehend me if you interpret the journey upward to be the ascent of the soul into the intellectual world according to my poor belief, which, at your desire, I have expressed—whether rightly or wrongly God knows. But, whether true or false, my opinion is that in the world of knowledge the idea of good appears last of all, and is seen only with an effort; and, when seen, is also inferred to be the universal author of all things beautiful and right, parent of light and of the lord of light in this visible world, and the immediate source of reason and truth in the intellectual; and that this is the power upon which he who would act rationally either in public or private life must have his eye fixed.

I agree, he said, as far as I am able to understand you.

Moreover, I said, you must not wonder that those who attain to this beatific vision are unwilling to descend to human affairs; for their souls are ever hastening into the upper world where they desire to dwell; which desire of theirs is very natural, if our allegory may be trusted.

Yes, very natural.

And is there anything surprising in one who passes from divine contemplations to the evil state of man, misbehaving himself in a ridiculous manner; if, while his eyes are blinking and before he has become accustomed to the surrounding darkness, he is compelled to fight in courts of law, or in other places, about the images or the shadows of images of justice, and is endeavoring to meet the conceptions of those who have never yet seen absolute justice?

Anything but surprising, he replied.

Anyone who has common sense will remember that the bewilderments of the eyes are of two kinds, and arise from two causes, either from coming out of the light or from going into the light, which is true of the mind's eye, quite as much as of the bodily eye; and he who remembers this when he sees anyone whose vision is perplexed and weak, will not be too ready to laugh; he will first ask whether that soul of man has come out of the brighter life, and is unable to see because unaccustomed to the dark, or having turned from darkness to the day is dazzled by excess of light. And he will count the one happy in his condition and state of being, and he will pity the other; or, if he have a mind to laugh at the soul which comes from below into the light, there will be more reason in this than in the laugh which greets him who returns from above out of the light into the cave.

That, he said, is a very just distinction.

But then, if I am right, certain professors of education must be wrong when they say that they can put a knowledge into the soul which was not there before, like sight into blind eyes.

They undoubtedly say this, he replied.

Whereas, our argument shows that the power and capacity of learning exists in the soul already; and that just as the eye was unable to turn from darkness to light without the whole body, so too the instrument of knowledge can only by the movement of the whole soul be turned from the world of becoming into that of being, and learn by degrees to endure the sight of being, and of the brightest and best of being, or in other words, of the good.

Very true.

And must there not be some art which will effect conversion in the easiest and quickest manner; not implanting the faculty of sight, for that exists already, but has been turned in the wrong direction, and is looking away from the truth?

Yes, he said, such an art may be presumed.

And whereas the other so-called virtues of the soul seem to be akin to bodily qualities, for even when they are not originally innate they can be implanted later by habit and exercise, the virtue of wisdom more than anything else contains a divine element which always remains, and by this conversion is rendered useful and profitable; or, on the other hand, hurtful and useless. Did you never observe the narrow intelligence flashing from the keen eye of a clever rogue—how eager he is, how clearly his paltry soul sees the way to his end; he is the reverse of blind, but his keen eyesight is forced into the service of evil, and he is mischievous in proportion to his cleverness?

Very true, he said.

But what if there had been a circumcision of such

natures in the days of their youth; and they had been
severed from those sensual pleasures, such as eating
and drinking, which, like leaden weights, were attached to them at their birth, and which drag them
down and turn the vision of their souls upon the
things that are below—if, I say, they had been released from these impediments and turned in the opposite direction, the very same faculty in them would
have seen the truth as keenly as they see what their
eyes are turned to now.

Very likely.

Yes, I said; and there is another thing which is
likely, or rather a necessary inference from what has
preceded, that neither the uneducated and unin-
formed of the truth, not yet those who never make an
end of their education, will be able ministers of State;
not the former, because they have no single aim of
duty which is the rule of all their actions, private
as well as public; nor the latter, because they will not
act at all except upon compulsion, fancying that they
are already dwelling apart in the islands of the blest.

Very true, he replied.

Then, I said, the business of us who are the found-
ers of the State will be to compel the best minds to
attain that knowledge which we have already shown
to be the greatest of all—they must continue to ascend
until they arrive at the good; but when they have as-
cended and seen enough we must not allow them to
do as they do now.

What do you mean?

I mean that they remain in the upper world: but
this must not be allowed; they must be made to descend again among the prisoners in the cave, and
partake of their labors and honors, whether they are
worth having or not.

But is not this unjust? he said; ought we to give

them a worse life, when they might have a better?

You have again forgotten, my friend, I said, the intention of the legislator, who did not aim at making any one class in the State happy above the rest; the happiness was to be in the whole State, and he held the citizens together by persuasion and necessity, making them benefactors of the State, and therefore benefactors of one another; to this end he created them, not to please themselves, but to be his instruments in binding up the State.

True, he said, I had forgotten.

Observe, Glaucon, that there will be no injustice in compelling our philosophers to have a care and providence of others; we shall explain to them that in other States, men of their class are not obliged to share in the toils of politics: and this is reasonable, for they grow up at their own sweet will, and the government would rather not have them. Being self-taught, they cannot be expected to show any gratitude for a culture which they have never received. But we have brought you into the world to be rulers of the hive, kings of yourselves and of the other citizens, and have educated you far better and more perfectly than they have been educated, and you are better able to share in the double duty. Wherefore each of you, when his turn comes, must go down to the general underground abode, and get the habit of seeing in the dark. When you have acquired the habit, you will see ten thousand times better than the inhabitants of the cave, and you will know what the several images are, and what they represent, because you have seen the beautiful and just and good in their truth. And thus our State, which is also yours, will be a reality, and not a dream only, and will be administered in a spirit unlike that of other States, in which men fight with one another about shadows only and are distracted in the struggle for power, which in their eyes is a great good. Whereas the truth is that the State in which the rulers are most reluctant to govern is always the best and most quietly governed, and the State in which they are most eager, the worst.

Quite true, he replied.

And will our pupils, when they hear this, refuse to take their turn at the toils of State, when they are allowed to spend the greater part of their time with one another in the heavenly light?

Impossible, he answered; for they are just men, and the commands which we impose upon them are just; there can be no doubt that every one of them will take office as a stern necessity, and not after the fashion of our present rulers of State.

Yes, my friend, I said; and there lies the point. You must contrive for your future rulers another and a better life than that of a ruler, and then you may have a well-ordered State; for only in the State which offers this, will they rule who are truly rich, not in silver and gold, but in virtue and wisdom, which are the true blessings of life. Whereas if they go to the administration of public affairs, poor and hungering after their own private advantage, thinking that hence they are to snatch the chief good, order there can never be; for they will be fighting about office, and the civil and domestic broils which thus arise will be the ruin of the rulers themselves and of the whole State.

Most true, he replied.

And the only life which looks down upon the life of political ambition is that of true philosophy. Do you know of any other?

Indeed, I do not, he said.

And those who govern ought not to be lovers of the task? For, if they are, there will be rival lovers, and they will fight.

No question.

Who then are those whom we shall compel to be guardians? Surely they will be the men who are wisest about affairs of State, and by whom the State is best administered, and who at the same time have other honors and another and a better life than that of politics?

They are the men, and I will choose them, he replied.

SELECTED BIBLIOGRAPHY

Botsford, G. W., and Robinson, C. A., Jr. *Hellenic History*. 4th ed. New York, 1956. A one-volume history of ancient Greece, with many photographs, maps, and plans.

Bowra, C. M. *The Greek Experience*. Cleveland, 1958. A masterly account of ancient Greece from the days of Homer to the fall of Athens in 404 B. C.

Burn, A. R. *Pericles and Athens*. New York, 1949. An interesting sketch of the great Athenian and his world.

Dinsmoor, W. B. *The Architecture of Ancient Greece*. London, 1950. The best scholarly treatment of the subject.

Finley, J. H., Jr. *Thucydides*. Cambridge, 1942. A brilliant interpretation.

Godolphin, F. R. B. (editor). *The Greek Historians*. 2 vols. New York, 1942. The complete works of Herodotus, Thucydides, Xenophon, and Arrian in a variety of translations.

Highet, G. *The Classical Tradition*. New York, 1949. A brilliant account of the chief ways in which the Græco–Roman tradition has shaped the literatures of modern Europe and America.

Jones, A. H. M. *Athenian Democracy*. New York, 1958. A fine, scholarly examination of Athenian government in the fifth and fourth centuries B. C.

Jowett, B. *The Dialogues of Plato Translated into English*. Introduction by R. Demos. 2 vols. New York, 1937. The famous translation of Plato, with an excellent introduction.

Kitto, H. D. F. *Greek Tragedy*. London, 1939. The best popular book on the subject.

Lawrence, A. W. *Greek Architecture*. London, 1957. An authoritative, general history of ancient Greek architecture.

Lullies, R., and Hirmer, M. *Greek Sculpture*. Translated by M. Bullock. Revised edition. New York, 1957. A magnificent picture book.

Oates, W. J., and O'Neill, E., Jr. (editors). *The Complete Greek Drama*. 2 vols. New York, 1938. All the extant Greek tragedies and comedies in a variety of translations.

Pfuhl, E. *Masterpieces of Greek Drawing and Painting*. Translated by J. D. Beazley. New edition. London, 1955. A beautiful picture book, with an authoritative text.

Richter, G. M. A. *The Sculpture and Sculptors of the Greeks*. New revised edition. New Haven, 1950. The best scholarly treatment of the subject, with over 750 photographs.

Robinson, C. A., Jr. (editor). *An Anthology of Greek Drama*. First Series. New York, 1949. Various translations of Æschylus' *Agamemnon,* Sophocles' *Œdipus the King* and *Antigone,* Euripides' *Medea* and *Hippolytus,* Aristophanes' *Lysistrata.*

———— (editor). *An Anthology of Greek Drama*. Second Series. New York, 1954. Various translations of Æschylus' *Prometheus Bound, Choëphorœ* and *Eumenides,* Sophocles' *Philoctetes* and *Œdipus at Colonus,* Euripides' *The Trojan Women* and *The Bacchæ,* Aristophanes' *The Clouds* and *The Frogs.*

———— (editor). *Selections from Greek and Roman Historians*. New York, 1957. Various translations from, among others, Herodotus, Thucydides, Xenophon, and Polybius.

Rodenwaldt, G., and Hege, W. *The Acropolis*. Norman, 1958. The buildings and sculptures of the Athenian

Acropolis, with a good text and extraordinarily beautiful photographs.

Taylor, A. E. *Plato: the Man and his Work.* New York, 1956. An excellent general study.

Toynbee, Arnold J. *Hellenism: the History of a Civilization.* New York, 1959. A stimulating study.

Warner, R. *The Greek Philosophers.* New York, 1958. An excellent popular account of Plato, Aristotle and others, with excerpts.

Zimmern, A. *The Greek Commonwealth: Politics and Economics in Fifth-Century Athens.* 5th ed. Oxford, 1931. A famous standard work.

INDEX

ATHENS

Index